CHAIRPEDIA
101 stories of chairs

LA FABRICA

Table of Contents

Drawing of chair profiles made by Erich Dieckmann (1896-1944) in the 1930s.

A Thousand and One Chairs

The *Chairpedia* is a collection of stories about chairs that began with the sedative and sedentary tales penned by writer Mauricio Wiesenthal for the book *Historias para leer sentado*, published by Andreu World as non-commercial edition in 2016. In his texts, we learned that César Ritz instructed his hotel decorators to make the furniture small so the rooms would look bigger, and that Rilke always wrote standing up and only sat down to read. We also discovered curious facts and anecdotes like the one about Justice Du Hellain, who asked to be buried with his chair, and others that made us eager to know more and ultimately inspired this new undertaking: a compilation of histories and stories to help spread "chair culture" in a more entertaining and less academic way.

Every chair has a story to tell, and there's room for all of them here—even those in which design doesn't play a fundamental role. There are one hundred and one chairs, but there might have been many more. If we could, we would have included a thousand and one chairs in this remarkable encyclopedic work. There is a lot to be said about the chair, as arguably the most iconic piece in the history of furniture, and that history can be told as precisely and factually as any other, but we decided to combine precision with an open, multifaceted approach by inviting a variety of experts—all qualified design, architecture, or art historians—from different generations and geographical locations to help us tell it. We enlisted their aid, not out of any desire to pontificate on the subject, but because we wanted to learn from the best and share that knowledge with readers.

The contents are divided into chapters whose titles offer another clue as to the nature of this publication. The selection of stories is entirely subjective: we chose these, but they could just as easily have been others, because there's no shortage of options. Using illustrations instead of photographs to accompany these texts was also a deliberate choice and a herculean undertaking for Antonio Solaz, who cleverly avoided monotony by multiplying his range of creative media and methods. We gave him complete freedom to interpret the stories as he saw fit, trusting that the result would be a genuine illustrated book in which form follows function, just as the Bauhausians said good chairs should do—the same kind of chairs Andreu World has been making for the past sixty-five years. The story of this firm is the last in the book, but it could just as easily have been the first. And now, let's take a seat and give thanks for this initiative.

Ramón Úbeda

101 stories of chairs

Popular Culture

Design Classics

Spanish Classics

Archetypes

Introduction

Sedative and Sedentary Tales

Mauricio Wiesenthal

The Heavenly Father's Wingback Chair

A good armchair is an unmistakable sign of authority. Once reserved for the man of the house, today women should announce the triumph of gender equality by claiming the fireside wingback chair. Oddly enough, the most famous wingback in history—made by an artisan from Turin named Renzo Frau, who launched his design in 1912—had a female name, "Poltrona Frau." Upholstered in smooth leather or *capitonnée*, Frau armchairs gave bourgeois homes an unforgettable style and became symbols of prosperity and power. Their advertising was also quite original: a poster of the Heavenly Father lounging in a chair, with a slogan that read, "And on the seventh day He rested... in a Frau easy chair."

Saint Attilanus in His Chair

As the Aragonese are peaceful, home-loving men, nothing could be more fitting than the typical *auroras* they sing in Tarazona to Saint Attilanus, the city's glorious patron saint, presenting the holy man seated in his chair:

Tarazona is filled with joy
for it has a son of faith and religion,
the glorious Attilanus,
who shelters us under his wing.
Blessed circumstance:
we have him seated in his
vchair in the very house
where he was born.

Introduction

Stylish Seats for "Royal Business"

In the medieval codex *Las Siete Partidas*, we read that Alfonso x used the same chamber for all royal affairs: councils, banquets, and even the most intimate "comforts." A 15th-century manual of etiquette for the crown prince's household, *El libro de la cámara*, explains that the privy was a room beside the bedchamber where all sorts of items were kept: food, toiletries, clothing, prayer books, and... a seat or square box containing the chamber pot.

Elizabeth I of England answered the call of nature on a special box locked with a key, so that none but the queen could use it. It was covered in crimson fabric, trimmed with gold studs and cording, and had a padded velvet seat.

In the seventeenth and eighteenth centuries, chamber pots were covered in damask (red, crimson, or blue), velvet, or carpeting, and some were even bound, like a valuable tome, in morocco leather. However, when her husband Henry II died, Catherine de' Medici had her close stool shrouded in mourning black. This may have been a bad omen for his successor, Henry III, who was assassinated while seated on his commode, with a blanket over his shoulders.

The Old Spanish Court and the Guardian of the Chair

During Spain's Golden Age, Spanish court etiquette was nearly as elaborate and convoluted as that of Franz Josef's Vienna. A virtuous Spanish lady always kept her feet out of sight. This courtly rule of conduct was so strictly enforced that merely mentioning the queen's feet was considered a serious offense. Perhaps this was owing to the influence of Semitic culture; and it is certainly true that Spanish monarchs were bound by the rules of the court as strictly as a high priest following the prescribed rituals of temple worship. For instance, it is said that Philip III nearly burned to death on one occasion: the courtier responsible for guarding the royal chair had abandoned his post, and no one else dared to come to his aid!

Naturally, etiquette was observed even in death. The Spanish custom of being buried in monastic habits led one French writer to express astonishment at the fact that "only priests and nuns die in Spain."

Sedative and Sedentary Tales

Mauricio Wiesenthal

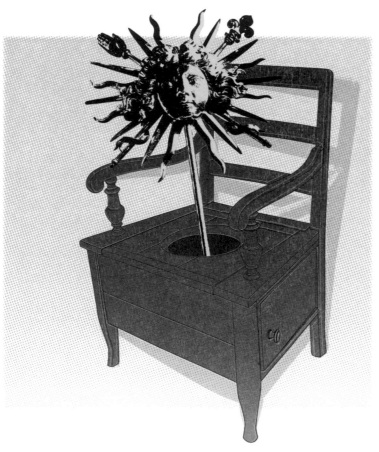

Louis XIV Announces His Marriage "On the Throne"

Shatterproof Glass: A Decisive Invention

The Palace of Versailles, where Molière had his great triumph, was designed as a fabulous stage, and the king spent his entire life in the spotlight. Louis XIV enjoyed living in the public eye so much that he opened his palace to anyone who wanted to witness the rituals of royal life, such as the king's daily awakening, luncheon, or strolls in the grounds. He even took the liberty of announcing his intention to marry Madame de Maintenon while seated on his "business chair" (a polite euphemism for the most basic amenity).

The royal chambers were accessible to anyone who could afford to rent a hat and sword and knew enough to keep quiet and bare his head in the monarch's presence. As it turned out, the king was too trusting; one day a thief strolled into the palace and made off with some curtains and tapestries.

The Marquise de Brézé, Cardinal Richelieu's sister, refused to sit down unless she was surrounded by cushions, because she was convinced that she had a glass bottom. This noble family produced more than its fair share of distinguished and deranged individuals. At the end of his life, Cardinal Richelieu believed he was a horse and would run laps around the billiard table while whinnying. His brother succumbed to the delusion that he was God the Father.

It seems that lunatics who believe they are made of glass—like Tomás Rodaja, the glass lawyer from Cervantes's tale—are less numerous now than in days of yore. Curiously, this mania diminished after the invention of shatterproof glass.

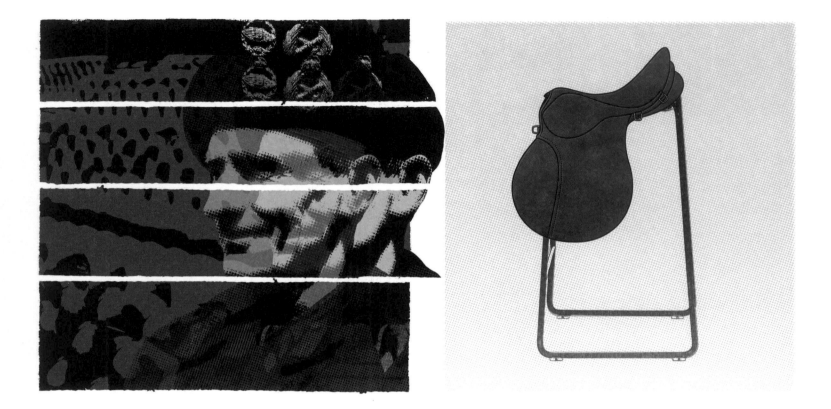

A Timely Stand in the House of Lords

The Spanish word for a parliamentary seat, *escaño*, comes from the Latin *scamnum*, meaning "bench," "stool," or "step." Not everyone can claim the privilege of sitting on the cushioned benches of the House of Lords, but Sir Bernard Montgomery, who defeated Field Marshal Rommel at El Alamein in 1942, had undoubtedly earned his seat. One day, he rose from his place on the red bench, turned to a lord sitting to his right and, with a composed face, quietly said, "I apologize for disturbing you, but I believe I am having a coronary." The doctors who examined him at the hospital concluded that he had indeed suffered a heart attack, and that he had stood up just in time.

Chairs of Geniuses

Salvador Dalí's shoe size was 41, but when he painted, he wore slippers several sizes too small—a 38, to be precise—to get his creative juices flowing. Discomfort stimulates ingenuity. At his Weimar home, Goethe wrote while sitting on a wooden sawhorse, similar to the pommel horses used by Olympic athletes. Rilke stood up to write, using a high lectern, and to recite, only sitting down to read. And the Achilleion—the palace built by Empress Sisi on Corfu—still contains the desk used by Kaiser Wilhelm II, with the peculiar saddle stool where he sat to write.

Sedative and Sedentary Tales

Mauricio Wiesenthal

Manuel de Falla's Chair Bunker

The Spanish composer Manuel de Falla was a great hypochondriac. He did not have a strong constitution, and he also suffered a number of minor ailments (migraines, indigestion, and rheumatism). He was so apprehensive that he even feared the hearty embraces with which the painter Zuloaga, a stocky Basque, would often greet him. Zuloaga recalled that when he visited Falla in Granada, the composer's sister warned him not to hug his friend because he was very weak. The painter found him barricaded behind a veritable bunker of chairs. Falla stretched out his hand, effectively warding off any attempt at an embrace, and said, "How do you do, Don Ignacio? As you can see, what with these headaches and my chronic illnesses, I am barely getting by: just so-so..."

A Chair for a Hat

One of the rules of Spanish etiquette when "paying a visit" was to show great reverence for the caller's hat. The Arab and Jewish ancestors on our family tree may explain why this eastern custom survived so long in Spain. "The civility shown to a private gentleman's hat," the great traveler Richard Ford observed, "is very marked among the formal gentry of the provinces; he is not allowed to hold it in his hand, nor to put it on the ground; the punctilious master of the house rushes at this cardinal type of gentility, seizes it, and, in spite of gentle resistance, cushions it on a chair by itself, or on the sofa-seat of honour. [...] The traveller, if he wishes to be *muy cumplido y muy formal*, complete and formal, which latter has not the priggish signification of our term, must remember, whenever a Spaniard to whom he desires to show attention calls upon him, to take his hat *nolens volens*, and seat it like a Christian on a chair of its own."

A Grave for a Chair

One of the most famous "imaginary invalids" was Justice Du Hellain. This magistrate, who spent his career in Caen, was quite apprehensive about his health and convinced himself that he was consumptive. Though outwardly he seemed quite hale and hearty, he refused to let anyone disturb his convalescence and remained seated in a chair, even when hearing cases. Later, he began to complain of migraines. The doctors told him that darkness and rest would lessen the pain, so Justice Du Hellain decided to take his repose even more seriously, remaining seated or lying in bed at all times. In his will, he stipulated that he was to be buried at night, in the same bed where he had expired, and that no one was to move his body or even change the bedding. And so, when he died in 1828, a large grave was dug in the cemetery of Caen, spacious enough to accommodate a chair, a bed, and the honorable justice in his pajamas and nightcap.

Knowing Where To Sit

Gore Vidal, the best-selling author of many renowned literary works (*Julian*, *Hollywood*, *Empire*, etc.), confessed that the secret of his media success was to sit beside an exotically or extravagantly dressed person at every party. In the absence of a Mohawk hairdo or a dazzling society woman, an Indian in a turban will do just as well.

"If you want to be on the front page of any newspaper anywhere," Vidal recommended, "you must always sit next to a man with a turban as he is bound to be photographed."

There are countless photographs of the famous writer beside a maharajah.

Sedative and Sedentary Tales

Mauricio Wiesenthal

The Chairs and Bathtubs of the Ritz Hotel

Hotel bathtubs became more comfortable thanks to Edward VII, who had a habit of bathing with his female friends. When the corpulent ruler complained that the tubs were too cramped, César Ritz decided to make them larger and more comfortable.

The clever Ritz had a solution for every problem. And just as he had the bathtubs made larger, he ordered the furniture made smaller for more intimate settings, like the bar on the Rue Cambon side of his luxurious hotel in Paris's Place Vendôme. As space was very limited, he told the decorators to use smaller tables and chairs so the venue would look and feel larger than it actually was.

Take Two Chairs

Charles de Morny was a famous French politician and banker related to the entire aristocracy (his stepbrother was Napoleon III). Speaking of his heritage, he once cynically remarked, "In my line, we have been bastards "de mère en fils" for three generations. I am a king's great-grandson, a bishop's grandson, a queen's son and an emperor's brother." He upheld the family tradition by siring numerous illegitimate children, some confirmed and others, like Sarah Bernhardt, the stuff of speculation and legend. He gave Zola the idea for the character of Monsieur de Marsy in the novel *His Excellency Eugène Rougon*.

Morny was reportedly quite absent-minded and even discourteous to his friends, in part because he considered himself a cut above everyone else due to his illustrious lineage, influence, and wealth. One day Baron Alfonso de Rothschild, a fellow banker and collector, came to call. When the baron entered the study, Morny did not look up and simply grunted, "Take a chair, sir," as he continued to write. "Do you know who I am?" the offended visitor exclaimed. "You are speaking to Alfonso James Rothschild!" "In that case," Morny replied, "will you please take two chairs."

Chairpedia

Popular Culture

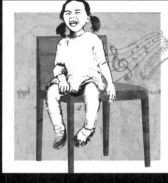

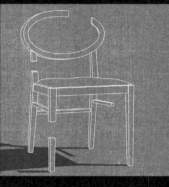

Design Classics

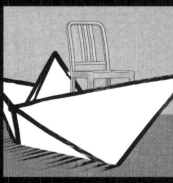

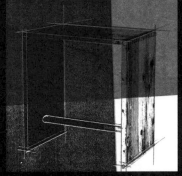

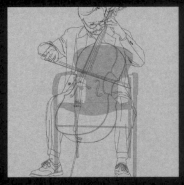

Archetypes

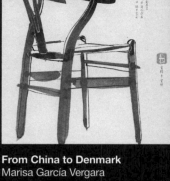

Seats of Power

Changing the World

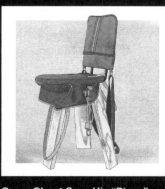

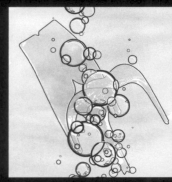

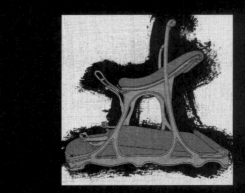

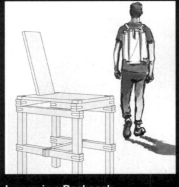

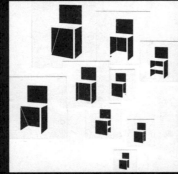
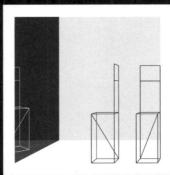

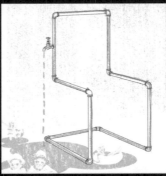

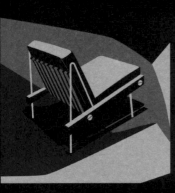
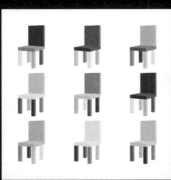

Chairpedia

Proust's Piles of Chairs
Daniel Cid
page 186

Pessoa's Chair
Daniel Cid
page 188

The Man Who Didn't Know How to Sit
Santi Barjau
page 190

Loos Sits on His Secrets
José María Faerna
page 192

A Chair for Dr. Freud
Daniel Cid
page 194

A Conversation on the Train
Isabel Campi
page 196

A Bucket Seat
José María Faerna
page 198

Chairs and Letters

Stevenson, Henry James, Two Chairs, and Five Tables
José María Faerna
page 202

Edgar Allan Poe's Ghostly Chairs
José María Faerna
page 204

A Privileged Chair
Patricio Sáiz
page 206

Neruda's Mediterranean Chair
Mónica Piera
page 208

Hergé and Prouvé
Oriol Pibernat
page 210

Chairness

Alberto Lievore's Chairness
Ramón Úbeda
page 214

A Chair Named Desire
Carmen Sevilla
page 216

50 Manga Chairs
Ana Domínguez
page 218

The Story of Andreu World
Ramón Úbeda
page 224

The Queen's Little Chair

By Isabel del Río

When I was a little girl, we played a game called "A la sillita de la reina" (To the Queen's Little Chair), a very resourceful form of amusement as it didn't require accouterments such as marbles, ropes, balls, jacks, or handkerchiefs. The game was quite simple: two girls joined hands (it worked best if they were crossed, right hand with right and vice versa), and a third girl sat on the "throne" formed by their interlocking arms, holding onto the necks of the other two as they swung her back and forth. It was a kind of race, where the "queen" and her "subjects" had to run to some distant goal while chanting a tune. Although there are many variations and versions of the song, it went something like this:

> *To the queen's little chair,*
> *she never washed or combed her hair.*
> *She used a comb one day*
> *Four hairs went astray:*
> *one, two, three, four...*
> *And the chair gave way!*

These popular games were passed down from one generation to the next, and no one knows how they got started, but now, in the midst of our booming technological revolution, they seem doomed to disappear. Thankfully, in 1560 Pieter Brueghel the Elder depicted more than eighty of these classic children's games, preserving them for posterity.

Musical Chairs

By Santi Barjau

In the game of musical chairs, participants walk around a circle of chairs while the music plays, and when it stops they scramble to find a seat... but there's always one chair less than the number of players. It's a simple game (every house has chairs, and all you need is a music player or someone who can play an instrument or even just carry a tune) and tends to create a lot of hilarious situations.

Even seats in the solemn temples of classical music occasionally provide entertaining anecdotes. This has probably happened to you: you're sitting in a concert hall, waiting for a piano concert to begin. The audience is hushed, expecting to see the pianist at any moment; suddenly, a figure appears on stage, and everyone simultaneously bursts into a vigorous round of applause. But then they realize their mistake: it's only the manager, come to lower or raise the bench or adjust its position... And when the soloist finally arrives, you patiently wait as s/he makes another series of vertical and horizontal adjustments, until the seat is just right (though it may have been just right to begin with) and the first notes are finally heard...

But I found my favorite musical chair at the Museu Maricel in Sitges. It's a chair with a hidden surprise: a built-in music box that is activated when someone sits on it. When I went with my family, the museum guide asked me to sit on it (I was the youngest), much to the delighted surprise of the group. On subsequent occasions, when I knew what to expect, I made a game of feigning surprise so as not to disappoint the old guide or ruin it for first-time visitors.

Silvio Rodríguez Sings a "Story of the Chair"

By Ramón Úbeda

Few artists sit down while singing on stage, but Silvio Rodríguez is one of them. Other exceptions include his compatriots Pablo Milanés and Noel Nicola, experts in Cuban Nueva Trova, or Spain's legendary Camarón de la Isla and his fellow flamenco singers. Phil Collins did it once while on tour in Chile, although it was only for health reasons. Some performers use a stool if the show is long and the years weigh heavily. Chairs are generally incompatible with rock, but not with poetry. Many feel that Silvio's ode to the chair, "Historia de la silla," is one of most beautiful songs ever composed by the Cuban singer-songwriter and poet. He wrote it in 1969 for his album *En vivo en Argentina*, a live recording made in April 1984 with Pablo Milanés in Buenos Aires just a few months after the military dictatorship ended. Unlike shoes, chairs are rarely mentioned in popular songs. Why? Your guess is as good as mine.

By the roadside stands a chair,
predators prowl in that place.
The friend's jacket hangs there,
he doesn't sit to slow his pace.
His shoes are worn to a shine so bright
they sear his throat in the sun.
And in his weariness an old man's
shadow dries the sweat that he has won.

On the point of love the friend travels,
the sharpest point you've ever seen.
A point that can dig holes in soil,
in ruins, or a woman's mien.
That's why he's a fighter and a lover,
that's why he's metal and wood.
That's why he sows roses and reasons
for flags and arsenals of statehood.

A man with a song will have torment,
a man with company, solitude.
A man who walks the right path will find
dangerous chairs inviting him to stop.
But the song is worth the torment,
and company worth the solitude.
The agony of haste is always worthwhile,
even when chairs overwhelm certitude.

"Quien fue a Sevilla perdió su silla"

By Ramón Úbeda

This phrase, which literally means "he who went to Seville lost his chair," is a popular saying that every Spanish child knows by heart. A rough English equivalent might be "Finders keepers, losers weepers." It's a great adage because it rhymes and teaches kids a graphic lesson about what to expect later in life. If you doze off or get distracted, you may find that someone else has taken your spot. There are other versions, like "Quien fue a Morón, perdió su sillón" (he who went to Morón lost his armchair), but actually the grammar is a bit off: it should be "he who left Seville lost his chair," because it's inspired by a historical event. During the reign of Henry IV (1454–1474), the archbishopric of Santiago de Compostela was granted to a nephew of Alonso de Fonseca, the Archbishop of Seville. The Galician town was a hotbed of unrest at the time, so the nephew asked his uncle if he would be willing to temporarily trade places and settle things down up north. When the uncle returned to Seville, he found his nephew firmly ensconced in the archbishop's chair and unwilling to relinquish his seat. Apparently, he found the hot sun and fried fish of the south more enjoyable than Galician empanadas and northern rains. In the end, the ousted cleric had to get a papal mandate and ask the king to intervene before he could recover his seat.

"N'hi ha per a llogar-hi cadires"

By Ramón Úbeda

In Catalan, as in so many other languages, there are some traditional sayings or expressions that simply can't be translated. This particular one, which literally means "you could even rent chairs for this," is used when someone behaves in a bizarre or unconventional way, and more correctly refers to extraordinary situations that create a sense of excitement or anticipation. It is derived from the phrase *s'hi llogaran cadires* ("chairs for rent"), once used by town criers to announce upcoming shows. It was a kind of sales pitch, because the fact that audiences were being offered a chair—even if they had to rent it—meant that the entertainment was worth seeing.

Portraying Chairs

By Oriol Pibernat

They're always abundant at old-timer's flea markets, and you can buy them easily and cheaply online. *Cartes-de-visite* and portraits for family albums began to appear in the mid-nineteenth century, although the majority date from the early 1900s. Many of these images have a peculiar commonality: the subjects are shown at full-length, sitting in or leaning on a chair.

The chair is a prop used to set the scene, a survival from the photographic portraits of distinguished men that first started the trend, where we can make out columns, draperies, and plants. These elaborate backdrops can be directly linked to Baroque-influenced pictorial prototypes. However, as studio portraits grew more popular and photographers' client bases expanded to include the middle class, such bombastic staging came to be viewed as pretentious and therefore ridiculous. And so, the chair became the last surviving prop of third-rate "court portraits"; a bourgeois aid for a mesocratic visual world; a pretense of elegance for the masses who flocked to have their portraits taken as professional photographers expanded their business and studios sprang up on every corner.

At the same time, chairs were associated with other conventions. In period portraits of couples, the woman was often seated, underscoring her passive role, while the man asserted his dominant position by standing. The same seating/standing conventions often applied to individual portraits as well. Bourgeois values were conveyed in every detail of the sitters' bodies—their placement, posture, pose, demeanor, and expression—as well as by their attire and accessories. And the chair is a perfect complement for a posed body: in addition to supporting and reinforcing a firm posture, it provides a decorative flourish and promotes decorum. However, with the occasional dash of mischief or extravagance, it can also serve to bend the rules. A chair may be an ordinary household item, but the type of chair chosen can be a telling indication of social status.

But let's forget about the social perspective and focus on what we see in those images. They were and are individual portraits, but how individual? They undoubtedly portray specific people. If we exercise our ability to scrutinize images and empathize with strangers, we can begin to detect singular human identities and imaginatively reconstruct events from their lives. Yet we should also remember that what we are seeing is the result of a process of visual standardization and the industrial proliferation of reproductions. The passing years and recycled existence of those portraits have erased emotional ties, biographical connections, and even a large part of their cultural identification. We know nothing about those individuals other than what we are able to imagine. The person-thing relationship itself seems to alter over time. Might this be because, with each passing year, we know less about the unique human beings in those portraits, and more about the features of the types of chairs pictured with them? What a paradox! Portraits were invented to immortalize and preserve the memory of people and personalities, not chairs.

In the Boudoir

By Santi Barjau

A poster designed by Marcello Dudovich for Borsalino, the famous manufacturer of men's hats, caused a sensation in 1911 Italy. The firm's luxury products, sold under the Zenit brand, were the ultimate symbols of an exclusive world of privilege that would disappear shortly afterwards with the outbreak of World War I. Dudovich's poster, rendered in shades of yellow, showed a Rococo chair with a derby hat, a pair of gentleman's gloves, and a walking stick. What were those accessories doing there? Who owned them? The elegant, refined setting told everyone exactly what the scene implied: a man of good social position (clearly a respectable bourgeois citizen, a married man, an upstanding pillar of the community) is visiting his *femme du monde* (secret lover, prostitute, or mistress). After hanging his coat on a lavish stand, or handing it to the lady's maid, he has apparently—with the liberty of one who knows he is safe in friendly, familiar territory—left his personal effects, including his exclusive Borsalino hat, on the chair and prepared to enjoy a pleasant evening.

The first modern advertising posters regularly used and abused images of women. Often the product was not even pictured, and the only ploy was a sinuous, seductive female figure. In the early twentieth century, German poster artists like Lucian Bernard created the *Sachplakat* or object poster, featuring nothing but an image of the product and the brand name against a neutral background. Dudovich's idea for this poster was innovative because he eliminated the man but still managed to suggest his presence.

The chair, which takes up most of the image, is merely a pedestal for displaying the hat like a trophy, a hat worn by elegant men who led lives of luxury and pleasure. This world of the *Belle Époque* soon gave way to other realities, and Marcello Dudovich adapted his posters to suit the new times.

Domingo the Carpenter

By Daniel Giralt-Miracle

In the 1960s, Ibiza was still an island paradise, barely touched by modernity, where the rural world thrived. That world included Domingo, an old carpenter, and his young nephew and assistant, who plied their trade in the Dalt Vila or "upper town." Domingo worked the solid wood of the island junipers, using saws, planes, rasps, chisels, and other traditional tools to shape it with consummate skill. In fact, his workshop produced many of the chairs and tables bought by members of the large colony of German, English, French, and American artists to furnish their homes on the island. These creative expats regularly exhibited at the Carl van der Voort Gallery, right across from the shop where Domingo spent his long workdays and was frequently interrupted by a friendly neighbor—none other than the famous architect Josep Lluís Sert—who stopped by to chat.

Many clients fell in love with the popular carpenter's furniture, and one was a German who happened to be the director of the Museum Angewandte Kunst in Frankfurt. Despite championing rationalism, functionalism, and *Gute Form*, this applied arts center did not hesitate to add Domingo's tables and chairs to its permanent collection, placing them alongside seats designed by Mies, Breuer, and Le Corbusier. Thanks to Domingo, an age-old Mediterranean cultural tradition is now part of the great history of European design.

The Chair from Its Invention to the Twentieth Century

By Isabel Campi

Today, beyond its basic functional definition, the chair has become the most designed cultural object in the Western world. By tracing the evolution of the chair, we can decipher the cultural, social, and technological history of an entire civilization. Even so, it took centuries for the chair to become an ordinary household item. According to some authors, the chair was not used by all social classes until the Renaissance, and true democratization came two hundred years later, for until the late eighteenth century the protocol of nobility dictated that chairs were reserved for the highest social and religious offices. As we will see, the chair was not a bourgeois invention, but we have the middle classes to thank for its widespread use and the countless configurations devised by designers and architects who became the arbiters of mass taste. The history of the chair, like that of any other piece of furniture, can be analyzed through the ages in light of four factors: its functional purpose; its ability to represent a social class or group; the technology used in its construction; and its integration with or independence from architecture.

Egypt
2300 BC
Egyptian chair

Greece
6th century BC
Klismos chair

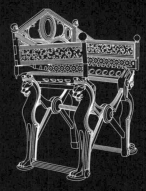

Middle Ages
8th century
Throne of Dagobert, France

A cultural object

Unlike other vertebrate mammals, human beings walk upright, using only their lower limbs. In order to develop the prehensile functions of their upper limbs, humans had to place their spines in a vertical position. This gave rise to a distinctive musculature (gluteal or buttock muscles) and a singular spinal curve (in the lumbar region), which are put under considerable stress when we walk. Our species has come up with different ways to relax the muscles of a back still relatively ill-adapted to that constant struggle against gravity. Africans learned to crouch for hours at a time, and in India people discovered different yoga positions that completely relax the muscles without the help of any manmade objects. Chairs are not essential to the survival of human beings. Nomadic cultures don't use them, and they were very rare in India, China, and Japan until these countries came into contact with the West. Even today, traditional Japanese houses are devoid of chairs, and at mealtimes people kneel at the table instead of sitting. The Eastern idea of comfort requires that people be able to control their muscles at all times, without relying on external aids. In contrast, the Western notion of comfort is based on furniture that ministers to the human body's need for relaxation.

Chairs in the ancient world

The chair started out as monument—or, more accurately, a throne at the heart of the sacred. Ancient kings and gods were pictured seated before a standing audience. Although this idea lost ground in Greek and Roman culture, it returned with a vengeance in the Byzantine Empire and the medieval period, spreading from civil to religious life: in the cathedrals, worshipers remained standing while mass was said.

We know exactly what the chairs of the Egyptian pharaohs were like, as archeologists have found intact specimens. These tell us that the oldest chairs displayed today in museums were richly decorated with precious materials such as gold, mother-of-pearl, and ebony.

The ancient Egyptians had sophisticated woodworking techniques that remained practically unaltered until the Middle Ages. They used saws and drills, but apparently it took them a while to discover the lathe, vestiges of which have been found in Etruria and Asia Minor from the seventh century BC. No seats have survived from ancient Mesopotamia, but Syrian and Persian stone reliefs seem to suggest that the ceremonial function of the chair was even more pronounced there than in Egypt. A relief carving in the Apadana of Persepolis, from the fifth century BC, shows the emperor seated on a raised throne (with turned spindles, by the way) and resting his feet on a stool, a custom also documented in medieval iconography. There are no extant examples of ancient Greek chairs, either, but painted vases and sculptures provide information about Hellenic furniture in general. These sources tell us they had two types of chairs.

One was the throne or seat of honor, imported from Egypt and Asia, reserved for ritual images in the temples or for magistrates, who had front-row seats carved from stone at the theaters.

The other was the *klismos*, a domestic chair that appears to be a purely Greek

The Chair form Its Invention to the Twentieth Century

Renaissance
15th century
Savonarola chair, Italy

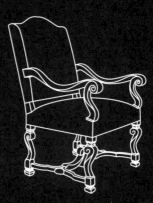

Baroque
17th centruy
Louis XIV, France

1850
No. 1 chair (1850)
Michael Thonet

invention with no Egyptian or Asian precedent. The reclined backrest and splayed legs allowed the body to adopt an agreeably relaxing position and gave the chair a delicate formal sense of balance.

The Roman Empire did not make any overly original contributions to chair design; Roman seat types were largely inherited from the Greeks, though they did show a strong predilection for luxury and flamboyance.

In everyday life, the Romans used different versions of the "barrel chair" invented by the Etruscans, and a folding stool known as the *sella curulis* or curule chair, symbol of the magistrates' authority, a design that became popular again during the Renaissance when it was known as the Savonarola chair. The ancient Romans apparently felt that reclining was a far more distinguished and elegant position than sitting. Diners lounged on couches around the table, and nobles and dignitaries appear on beds in their tombs. From a design perspective, more attention was paid to beds than to chairs, a curious phenomenon that endured until the eighteenth century.

The Middle Ages

The medieval way of life and stylistic production was inevitably influenced and shaped by the fall of the Roman Empire and its consequences: barbarian invasions, economic instability, wars, political violence, and corruption.

Medieval monarchs and landowners led a nomadic existence, partly because they were constantly at war, but also because moving from castle to castle made it easier to keep a close eye on their domains and secure provisions. Naturally, the lord's furniture traveled with him. Some medieval chairs were well crafted and richly decorated, but for the most part they were crudely made. In an age of constant perils and temporary dwellings, people preferred to spend money on multipurpose, travel-friendly furniture. Luxury and ostentation were expressed by covering the walls in rich tapestries and brocades. A curious bronze folding chair of Roman inspiration has survived from this period, called the Throne of Dagobert after the Merovingian King of the Franks who owned it (seventh/eighth century).

The austerity of civil furniture contrasts with the opulence of its ecclesiastical counterpart. Richly carved choir stalls were built in Gothic cathedrals, and illuminated manuscripts or codices depicted saints and prophets seated on magnificently decorated *cathedrae*.

Renaissance, Baroque, and Rococo

According to Giedion, the first chairs to be considered standard household items were those used to furnish the Palazzo Strozzi in Florence (1490), which implies that by this date, at least in Italy, the chair had ceased to be a ceremonial rarity and was widely used. Even so, it would be quite some time before chairs became popular enough to replace benches and stools as the seating of choice at banquets.

The Renaissance grammar of ornament drew heavily on classical Antiquity and spread far and wide thanks to the invention of the printing press. Nevertheless, regional differences became more pronounced in the sixteenth century, giving rise to the first truly "national models." In Spain, the upper classes were slow

1860
Shaker (1820–1870)
United States

1870
Windsor
Great Britain

1880
Chippendale

to adopt the Italian custom of sitting in chairs; apparently women still preferred to sit on cushions arranged on a dais, in the Moorish style. However, the Spanish Renaissance did produce an austere, distinctive armchair whose design has survived intact to the present day.

The late sixteenth century brought important innovations in chair construction, such as the use of upholstery or the swivel chair, apparently imported from France. The explanation lies in the fact that builders had specialized and formed different guilds: carpenters, turners, joiners, cabinetmakers, etc. Consequently, in the seventeenth and eighteenth centuries chair design reached unprecedented heights of sophistication, luxury, and extravagance. In addition, trade with overseas colonies facilitated a steady supply of exotic woods, abundant silver, and a knowledge of new decorative techniques like lacquerwork or japanning.

For a long time, beginning in the seventeenth century, France set the standards of taste and style for the Western world. The court of Louis

xiv brought the *fauteuil* into vogue, an upholstered chair with a high back, made possible in part because high, stiff Spanish ruffs had fallen out of fashion. Despite all these novelties, the French court could not change certain long-ingrained habits. Nobles continued to cart their household belongings with them wherever they went, which explains the enduring popularity of *pliants* (folding chairs) and *tabourets* (stools), the persistent hierarchic use of chairs (at least in formal settings), and the fact that social life still revolved around the bedroom. Monarchs and aristocrats often received visitors and handled affairs of state in bed, and meals were served on folding tables and chairs carried in by servants. The concept of the dining room, as a space separate from the kitchen and the bedroom and the hub of social life, is a bourgeois invention that did not appear until the late eighteenth century.

The Rococo, an artistic and stylistic period often disdained as a late and quasi-decadent derivative of the Baroque, nevertheless introduced a revolutionary notion of comfort with important consequences for

chair design. Giedion says that, in the matter of postural comfort, eighteenth-century France picked up where ancient Greece left off.

Curved, upholstered backrests and cabriole legs supported the body in a way that allowed people to sit comfortably and facilitated relaxed, flexible social interactions.

Upholstery became indispensable and inspired a wide variety of models based on the *bergère* type. This period witnessed the birth of the *chaise courante*, a light portable chair that could be placed in the middle of the room when needed, and the *chaise meublant*e, usually lined up against a wall, which served a more decorative than practical purpose.

Another important Rococo contribution was the idea of the chair, and furniture in general, as part of a larger decorative program. Furniture makers, upholsterers, catalogue publishers, and architects worked together to create a harmonious whole, efficiently coordinating their various tasks and skills.

The Chair from Its Invention to the Twentieth Century

1890
Bugatti chair (1895)
Carlo Bugatti

1900
Barrel chair (1904)
Frank Lloyd Wright
Cassina

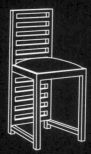

1910
Chair for the guest bedroom at
78 Derngate (1916)
Charles R. Mackintosh

The chair in the Industrial Age

The French obsession with beauty and elegance and the organization of builders into specialized guilds, as mentioned above, made it easy to cater to the tastes of the new ruling class: the bourgeoisie.

The first half of the nineteenth century witnessed an endless parade of new styles. The Rococo was followed by the Neoclassical, and fast on its heels came the Empire style, which found one of its most authentic expressions in Germany and Austria, where Biedermeier furniture offered a sophisticated reinterpretation of classicism. All these styles produced chairs of undeniable elegance and inspired a formal repertoire of designs that have remained popular to this day, especially their English versions. For all its variety of styles, however, this period did not contribute much in the way of new types.

The real breakthrough came with the technological novelties of the Industrial Revolution in the second half of the century. The Austrians invented springs; furniture makers discovered the constructive possibilities of metal, especially for outdoor furniture; and *papier maché* became a popular decorative material. The greatest structural innovation of this period came from the Central European furniture industry, which began investigating the myriad industrial applications of steam-bent wood in the mid-nineteenth century. The most iconic chair of this era is Michael Thonet's No. 14 chair (1859), an industrial piece that represented a clear departure from precedent, and a valuable lesson in the wisdom of adapting a form to a specific use and material. The vernacular industries of the day also created new types from which many modern models are derived, such as the Chiavari chair (Liguria, Italy), the British Windsor chair, and the exquisite pieces made by Shaker communities in the United States.

Yet the prosperous middle class was relentless in its demand for new styles, even if they were simply adulterated versions of Gothic, Isabelline, or Baroque standards. The nineteenth century failed to develop its own distinctive stylistic identity, instead preferring to cheapen those of earlier periods and falling into pure historicism. This confusion was exacerbated by the gradual disappearance of traditional artisans and craftsmen, disoriented by the pressure of new industrial working conditions based on productivity. When the signs of this disorientation became apparent, John Ruskin, William Morris, and others raised their voices in protest, denouncing—in word and in deed—the Victorian commercial design being produced in England and Europe, which had reached a low point at the Great Exhibition of 1851 in London. Ruskin, Morris, and the generation that came after them, the Arts and Crafts movement, wanted to promote the creation of a new artisanal concept of design inspired by the traditions of rural England. Arts and Crafts designers proclaimed a new ethics of design based on unity in labor, form adapted to function, constructive honesty, and natural and medievalizing inspiration. At the end of the century, this doctrine gave birth to the last great historical style: Art Nouveau.

Instead of historicism, Art Nouveau proposed a highly coherent, naturalistic style that was widely

1920
B302 (1927)
Le Corbusier, Jeanneret, and Perriand
Cassina

1930
"31" armchair, laminated beechwood (1932)
Alvar Aalto
Artek

1940
LCM (1946)
Charles and Ray Eames
Vitra

imitated around the world. Even so, there were two clearly differentiated schools: Belgium, France, and Spain developed an extravagant curvilinear brand of modernism inspired by the plant kingdom that gave wooden chairs a three-dimensionality which was highly unusual and definitely ill-suited to their structural purpose, though in some cases—Gaudí's chairs and benches, for example— it did produce surprisingly intuitive functional results. In contrast, the Jugendstil style that emerged in Germany and Austria was less whimsical and more intellectual. Austria was one of the leading European centers of industrial chair production, for by the turn of century it already had dozens of bentwood manufacturers. Today, the pieces designed by Viennese architects Josef Hoffmann, Otto Wagner, and Gustav Siegel for the Wiener Werkstätte and Jacob & Josef Kohn are still greatly admired for their formal purity and honest construction. The sophisticated chair collections of Scottish architect Charles R. Mackintosh, who worked in Glasgow in the early twentieth century in contact with the Viennese school, are also held in great esteem nowadays.

Chairs in the twentieth century

Strictly speaking, the aesthetic revolution of chair design in the twentieth century did not begin until after World War I, when the last vestiges of Art Nouveau and other historical styles were finally swept away by the vitality of the avant-garde movements. The twentieth century produced more structural and formal innovations than the twenty previous centuries.

Decorators and upholsterers were replaced by architects and industrial designers, professionals who saw the chair as a functional, spatial, and technological problem and proposed radically innovative solutions. The past century witnessed the creation of several new styles (what we might consider national variants of the Modern Movement), but the most interesting development was actually the range of brand-new types that emerged, types with no ancient or recent historical precedents. This typological revolution was triggered by the appearance of new methods and materials, as well as new social phenomena. In addition to being an important element in the home, the

chair had become a fixture at the workplace. Long days spent in front of a typewriter, a control panel, or a computer called for a thorough analysis of how to mitigate the stress of a sedentary position. Large gatherings, concert halls, stadiums, and associations also needed specific types of seats. Having inherited a certain sense of comfort and efficiency, advanced industrial societies were no longer content to have a few models of chairs for everything; they wanted a particular seat for each activity, whether in the domestic, professional, or social sphere.

The first radical attack on chair typology was launched by a Dutch designer named Rietveld. Even working with such a traditional material as wood, his Red Blue and Zig-Zag models managed to dissect the chair and reduce it to basic planes, giving the impression that it had been disembodied. The next great leap was made in the 1920s by Le Corbusier and the Bauhaus architects Marcel Breuer, Mart Stam, and Mies van der Rohe, who brilliantly applied tubular technology to seat construction.

The Chair from Its Invention to the Twentieth Century

1950
Tulip chair (1956)
Eero Saarinen
Knoll

1960
Sacco chair (1968)
Gatti, Paolini and Teodoro
Zanotta

1970
Wiggle side chair (1972)
Frank O. Gehry
Vitra

Perhaps the most unusual type is the cantilever chair, with a formal and constructive suitability as yet unsurpassed by any other metal chair. Finnish architect Alvar Aalto came up with a brilliant version of this archetype by exploring the possibilities of pressure-treated plywood, managing to adapt chair design to the ideological premises of the Modern Movement without incorporating its signature mechanical frigidity.

Immediately after World War II, the most radical novelties appeared in the United States, where Mr. and Mrs. Eames were employed by a powerful postwar industry eager to apply the results of wartime research to chair production. Initially they experimented with the plywood used by the aviation industry, and later they pioneered the use of molded and reinforced plastic and synthetic upholstery. In the 1950s, Charles and Ray Eames made important innovations in domestic chair design, but they also developed a wide range of cast aluminum models for office use. The Cranbrook Academy of Art brought together a group of designers (the Eameses, Eero

Saarinen, Harry Bertoia, and Florence Knoll) who created genuine design classics, combining bold technical experimentation with an organicist style far removed from the Bauhausian coldness of the interwar years.

In the 1960s and 70s, Italian designers made more than a few contributions to the world of chairs. They, better than most, captured the essence of the Pop art that had emerged in the English-speaking world the decade before and turned it into objects. The glorification of consumer culture, which Pop painters cynically extolled using the hyper-realism of advertising and comics, convinced a young and trusting public to accept plastic in the living room, along with its loud colors and shiny finishes. By collaborating with designers like Joe Colombo, Gae Aulenti, and Anna Castelli, among others, the firms Knoll, Artemide, and especially Kartell took the chair to the highest rung on the evolutionary ladder: a piece that could be assembled in a few seconds and required no finish or maintenance. Experimentation with synthetic materials and the appearance of young consumers led

to totally groundbreaking designs, such as inflatable PVC seats, beanbag armchairs, and chairs made of carved foam. In Denmark, Verner Panton took the Pop trend to its logical conclusion with interiors decorated in psychedelic colors and synthetic materials, for which he designed furniture like the Panton Chair (1959 and later). Although this chair gives the illusion of impossible balance and looks quite whimsical, it was actually based on an exhaustive study of how to mold plastic in one piece.

Pop paved the way for postmodernism by making a clean break with the modernist credo. As the 1980s dawned, designers turned away from the ideas of functionality, rejection of history, and technological optimism that had characterized the Modern Movement. New values focused on poetry, nods to historical styles (whether ancient or modern), and the revival of craftsmanship. The 1980s ushered in a period of frenetic formal experimentation with the chair that was not followed by an equally energetic technical and typological experimentation. The greatest achievement was managing to define a highly

1980
Rover chair (1981)
Ron Arad
Vitra

1990
Coast chair (1999)
Marc Newson
Magis

2000
Favela chair (2002)
Campana brothers
Edra

distinctive, colorful patchwork style riddled with references to the past and often infused with a delicate sense of humor and irony. For example, Robert Venturi's chairs for Knoll (1980), though reminiscent of consecrated furniture styles—Queen Anne, Chippendale, Empire, Sheraton, etc.—were made from cut plywood and decorated with painted motifs. Meanwhile, in Italy, Alessandro Mendini and the Memphis group reinterpreted avant-garde models in what they called a "neo-modern" style.

After nearly three decades of frenzied searching for new styles, the 1990s seemed to inaugurate an era of calm and serenity. However, it was not devoid of innovation, for a new design tool arrived on the scene: computer programs that made it possible to model three-dimensional curves. Designers also incorporated materials that defied our preconceived notions of their properties and abilities— flexible ceramic, metal foam, shape memory alloys—and, above all, conductive, lightweight, transparent, and semi-transparent plastics. The result was a wide range of plastic or tube chairs whose highly

streamlined, sensual lines made those of earlier periods seem coarse and heavy in comparison. This was the case of the Tom Vac stackable chair by Ron Arad (1997) the magnesium Go chair by Ross Lovegrove (1998), the entire series of chairs Philippe Starck designed for Kartell, Alberto Meda's office chair for Vitra (1996), and the Coast chair by Marc Newson for Magis (1999).

The close of the twentieth century was marked by a concern that still haunts us today, threatening the very future of humanity: the environmental crisis. This preoccupation inspired designers like the Campana brothers, Marcel Wanders, and Patricia Urquiola to go against the flow of hyper-technological, delocalized design, using warm, locally sourced materials such as wicker, textiles, and wood to express their desire to live in harmony with nature.

Isabel Campi originally wrote this text for a special issue of *ARDI* magazine titled "¡Siéntate!" [Sit Down!]. It was published in 1989, and she has taken this opportunity to extend the narrative to the end of the twentieth century. A new chapter is being added to the history of the chair as we move into the twenty-first century, a few glimpses of which are provided in this book. And each has its own story to tell.

The Best Chair

By Daniel Giralt-Miracle

Raül, an industrial designer born and educated in Barcelona but with a master's degree from the Royal College of Art in London, and his wife Candelaria, an interior designer from Gran Canaria, wanted to give their daughter something for her house as a wedding present. Asked what she would like, Helena replied that she wanted a chair for her desk. She left the choice up to them, asking only that they find the best chair possible: the most practical, the most ergonomic... and the most modern. Searching for the perfect seat, her parents refreshed their knowledge by poring over catalogues, visiting stores and factories, and recalling their visits to the London Design Museum and the Vitra Design Museum in Weil am Rhein. They also sought advice from their friend Fernando Amat, architect of the legendary and now defunct decoration boutique Vinçon, and reviewed the book *Arquitecturas diminutas. Diseños de arquitecto en el siglo xx* by Juli Capella, but they still couldn't find something that convinced them both. A consensus was finally reached when a friend told them he'd spotted a bargain at the Encantes market in Barcelona. For the ridiculously low price of one hundred and fifty euros, they could buy a genuine Thonet, certified by the label on the back: *Gebrüder Thonet. Möbel aus gebogenem Holze. I. Stefansplatz. Wien. Telephon 13275.* Raül and Candelaria rushed over to Stall 68 at the splendid market in Plaça de les Glòries, where they haggled with the vendor until he finally agreed to sell them the chair for one hundred euros. The happy couple carefully wrapped the gift and took it over to their daughter's house. Helena, who knew how her parents had agonized over the decision, eagerly unwrapped the package and exclaimed, "Oh, it's fabulous! It's just like the one Grandfather and Grandmother had in their entry hall, and I always longed for it, especially since theirs ended up in a bonfire one St. John's Eve!"

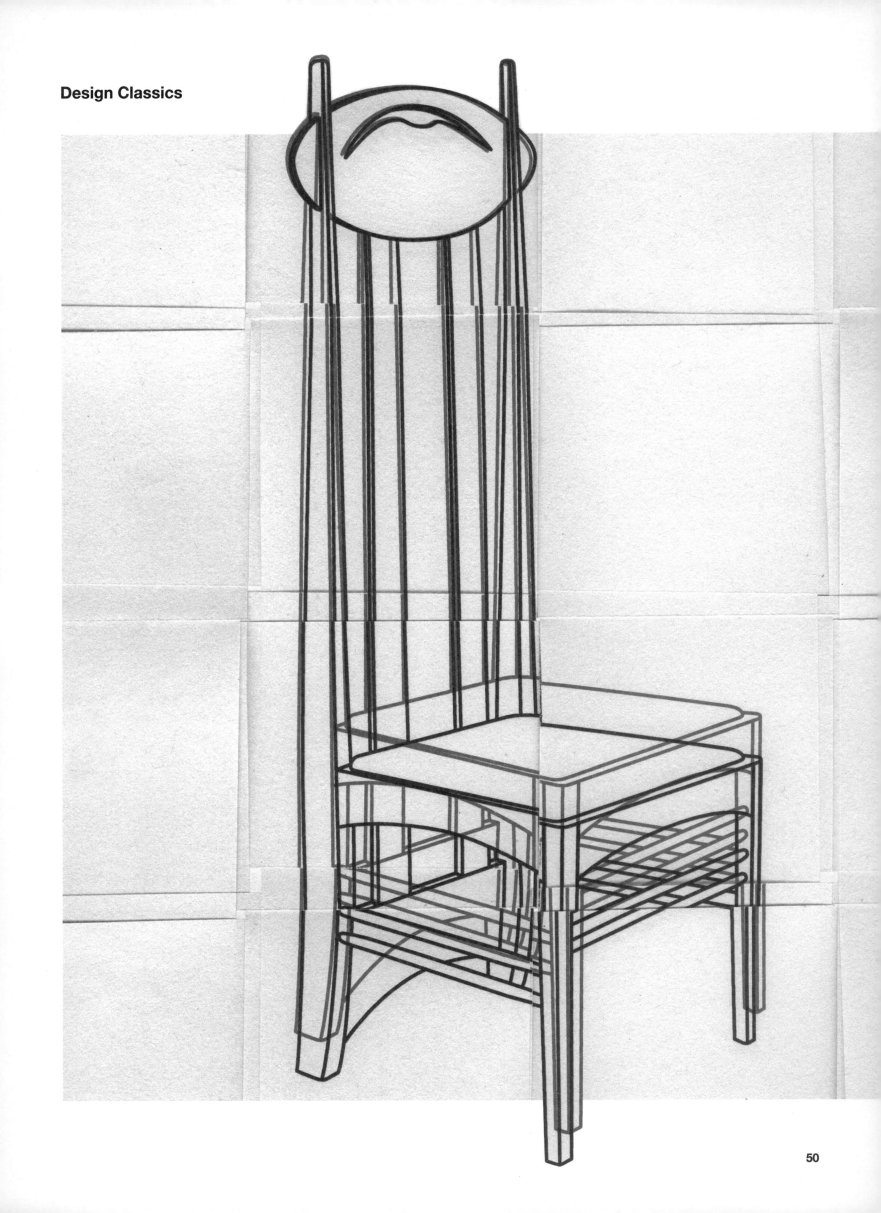

A Teatime Chair

By Isabel del Río

The extravagant Miss Catherine Cranston decided to open her first tearoom at 114 Argyle Street in Glasgow, Scotland. It was destined to be the first in a chain of lavishly appointed establishments, where elegant ladies could meet without the need for male company. The one on Argyle Street was an immediate success thanks to its billiards room, card room, smoking room, and ladies' tearoom. The enterprising Miss Cranston, a hard-nosed businesswoman, wanted to offer a teetotal alternative to the pubs that had taken over the city.

Years later, on the occasion of her marriage, she received the entire Argyle Street building as a wedding present. She decided to enlarge the tearoom and hired George Walton and Charles Rennie Mackintosh to decorate it. Walton was in charge of the wall murals, fireplaces, billiards, and electric lights, while Mackintosh handled the furnishings. And so Mackintosh, an architect who became the leading Scottish representative of Art Nouveau, designed the first of the unusually high-backed chairs that were destined to be his trademark.

The chairs created for the Argyle Street dining room were intensely modern, incorporating the Gothic inspiration of the Arts and Crafts movement begun by William Morris and the delicate curves of the modernist style. The chairs were made of oak, stained and varnished in black, with horsehair upholstered seats. The back had two slats on each side that tapered to a point, emphasizing its vertical lines. The headrest was a wooden oval pierced with the stylized outline of a bird in flight.

This must have been one of Mackintosh's favorite chairs, as he used it to decorate the house he shared with his wife and collaborator Margaret Macdonald, whom he had met when they were both students at the Glasgow School of Art.

The same design, known today as the Argyle chair, was later shown at the Eighth Exhibition of the Vienna Secession (1900) in the "Scottish room," a simple yet highly eloquent setting designed by the "Glasgow Four": Charles Rennie Mackintosh, the sisters Margaret and Frances Macdonald, and Herbert MacNair. That interior was so successful that it had a tremendous influence on the Wiener Werkstätte, a group of artists, architects, and designers established in Vienna in the early twentieth century.

Rietveld, Groenekan, and the "Antecessor" Chair

By José María Faerna

Gerard van den Groenekan must have been barely fourteen or fifteen years old in the winter of 1917/18 when he was taken on as an apprentice at the workshop that Gerrit Rietveld—a cabinetmaker and draftsman, according to city records—had opened on Utrecht's Adriaen van Ostadelaan in May. According to Gerard, the first version of the chair that marked the birth of modern furniture was made at that workshop in the summer of 1918. To celebrate this breakthrough, Rietveld posed before his shop window, proudly lounging in the chair with his employees gathered around like a modern-day praetorian guard, in the now-famous photograph that has since been reproduced a thousand times. Although some claim the chair was actually invented in 1916, Gerard's testimony has the ring of truth because we see him there, to the left of his master, smiling and leaning against the windowsill. This chair—or, more accurately, armchair—is usually seen as a symbol, a kind of prototypical manifesto of the Neo-Plastic ideas of the De Stijl movement applied to furniture: seven rectangular-section horizontal slats, six square-section vertical slats, and two panels that intersect freely in space without disrupting it, retain their own individual forms and basic properties when assembled, and become practically invisible when someone sits down. The early versions, like the one in that photo, had two wooden planks under the arms, but these were soon eliminated to heighten the sense of spatial continuity.

At the time, Rietveld knew little about art and was not prone to theoretical musings. More than Theo van Doesburg or Mondrian, his primary source of inspiration was the abstractions of naturalistic figures being developed in those years by Bart van der Leck, a less prominent member of the De Stijl group. The idea of this chair as a kind of laboratory experiment contrasts sharply with the workaday atmosphere of the photo, with everyone garbed in smocks and aprons like the honest, hard-working carpenters they were. Scholars try to trace this lineage back to Wright and Berlage, but they overlook another, plainly empirical genealogy: in the year 1900, when he was just a boy, Rietveld began working at the Poorstraat shop owned by his father, a cabinetmaker named Johannes Cornelis Rietveld. Following this genealogical line takes us back to 1908 and the Vertical chair, where Rietveld experimented with reducing the chair to its minimum material essence long before De Stijl came on the scene.

However, the search does not end there; we must go back a few more years to when Baron Van Tuyll van Serooskerken decided to renovate the gatehouse of Zuylen Castle, and Rietveld senior gave his son the simple task of creating a modest table with four chairs. The chairs were straight, monastic affairs, with cross-stretchers reinforcing the legs and a practically open back, outlined by fluted side posts and a splat one-third the width of the chair. The top rail was a triangular-section slat whose ends were slightly longer than the frame, timidly hinting at the virtual extension into space that would characterize every element of his 1918 chair. This plain, unpainted chair, like the one shown in the photograph of Adriaen van Ostadelaan, would not acquire its characteristic palette of red and blue with yellow ends until around 1925. The Zuylen chair is the *Australopithecus* of the avant-garde, the "Antecessor" species of the genus Chair. Like the Baby Jesus, it was born in a humble setting and raised by a carpenter, though Rietveld went on to become a designer and architect. Good old Groenekan, on the other hand, never became anything else. He worked with Rietvald for many years, patiently assembling his chairs, and continued doing so after the master's death until his own in 1989. Even after Cassina acquired the rights to the Red Blue chair, they gave him permission to keep making it for museums and private clients. Photographs taken in his final years show him as a happy old man, still wearing his smock.

From War to Peace

By Isabel Campi

The LCW (Lounge Chair Wood) is often called the "potato chip chair," a reference to American fast-food culture that might make us think it was the brainchild of a Pop designer, but nothing could be further from the truth. In 1945, Pop art was still a thing of the future: World War II was drawing to a close, and U.S. industries were busy churning out materials to support the war effort. It was no time for frivolity. This chair is the product of Charles and Ray Eames's efforts to master the art and technique of working with plywood when they opened a studio in Los Angeles, which had become an important aviation industry hub during the war. Plywood—thin layers or plies of wood glued together cross-grain under pressure—was used to make aircraft parts, splints for broken limbs, and litters. Strictly speaking, it was not a new material, but wartime research significantly enhanced its useful properties.

Mr. and Mrs. Eames took on the challenge of designing a chair made entirely of plywood. However, after countless experiments, they reached the conclusion that the seat and back could not be made in one piece, as it put too much stress on the plywood. So they split it into two pieces, joined by a curved spine and supported by two legs shaped like an upside-down U. The result is highly sculptural but also quite comfortable, because the curves and flexibility of the material adapt to the human body and allow a degree of movement. The Eameses managed to turn a material used for war into a memorable chair for peace.

The Navy Chair and Betty Grable's Derrière

By Ana Domínguez

The history of the Navy chair is one of the most surprising and amusing anecdotes I've ever heard. During World War II, the U.S. Navy had a problem: the chairs aboard its vessels weren't built to last several months at sea among rough sailors. The Navy urgently needed chairs that were sturdy yet lightweight, non-magnetic, impervious to the corrosion caused by sea salt, and fireproof to boot. A very tall order—but, as it turned out, not impossible. In the 1940s, Wilton C. Dinges, founder of Emeco, worked with an admiral to manufacture chairs from recycled aluminum and develop an amazing 77-step process which, combined with manual labor, made the finished products so indestructible that they came with a 155-year warranty.

Gregg Buchbinder, whose father bought this factory in the 1970s and later passed it on to him, was in New York one day, presenting a new chair he'd created with Philippe Starck, when he ran into Sir Terence Conran, the legendary interior decorator. He told me that Conran shared an unexpected and astonishing story: apparently, the curved seat of the 1006 Navy chair was modeled on Betty Grable's legendary backside! According to him, the most famous pin-up girl of the 1940s generously lent her "cheeks" to give it shape. The flabbergasted Gregg immediately called up his most senior employee, Davey Lake, who had worked at the factory his entire life. Lake confirmed that the rumor had been spread back in the day as a way of encouraging the sailors to be gentler with their chairs. Talk about the power of an illusion!

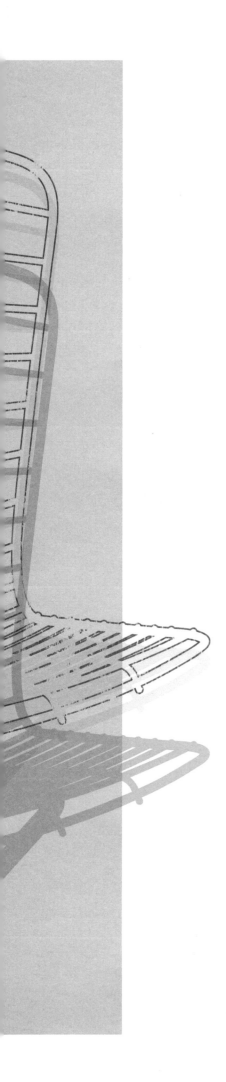

An American Icon on the Socialist Island

By Guillem Celada

In the heart of modern Havana, in the Vedado district, lies La Rampa, a popular stretch of Avenida 23 that experienced cultural splendor before the revolution, with cabarets like the Turquino and Las Cañitas at the Hotel Hilton Habana (now Hotel Habana Libre), and afterwards, when the revolutionary project was sexier.

In the 1960s, this area hosted the Congress of the International Union of Architects (1963), for which the Brutalist Cuban Pavilion was built. Every Saturday night at the "magic showcase", Fernando Ayuso presented his latest fashion designs with models strutting to the rhythms of the Grupo de Experimentación Sonora, an experimental band from the ICAIC (Cuban Institute of Cinematographic Art and Industry); and the painter Raúl Martínez covered the walls of a coffee shop with Pop murals that disappeared under a coat of paint a few years later.

In the midst of this bustling avenue stands the Coppelia ice cream parlor, known as the ice-cream cathedral thanks to the film *Strawberry and Chocolate*. The building that houses it is a stellar example of concrete architecture adapted to the Caribbean climate designed by architect Mario Girona, where half-open, partly covered indoor and outdoor spaces flow together. In the establishment's many spaces, seating is supplied by hundreds of Bertoia chairs, a wire chair model designed by Harry Bertoia for Knoll in 1952: specifically (I gather), the 1955 version with a special treatment for outdoor use.

Havana's Coppelia boasts the largest existing collection of this type of chair, but given that the parlor was built in 1966, I wondered if it was actually Harry's original model. Digging through the archives of the Cuban capital, I came across an advertisement for this design in an architectural journal from 1955, when Knoll had at least one distributor in Havana. As an American company, one would assume that Knoll stopped shipping its products to the island shortly after the revolution began.

The amount of wear and tear these seats have endured for more than fifty years is unimaginable. The lines at this massive ice cream parlor are legendary in Havana. Millions of customers have plumped down in them to enjoy their frozen treats. If they are original Knoll chairs, the fact that they've survived is irrefutable proof of superb workmanship. And even if they're local knockoffs, their hardiness is no less impressive.

The amazing thing is that, when the exhausted chairs finally do succumb after decades of intensive use, exposure to the elements, multiple coats of paint, and welding repairs, Cuban ingenuity, honed by necessity, gives them new dimensions in another design exercise with a healthy dose of intuition, evidence of which can be seen in the vicinity of the iconic landmark.

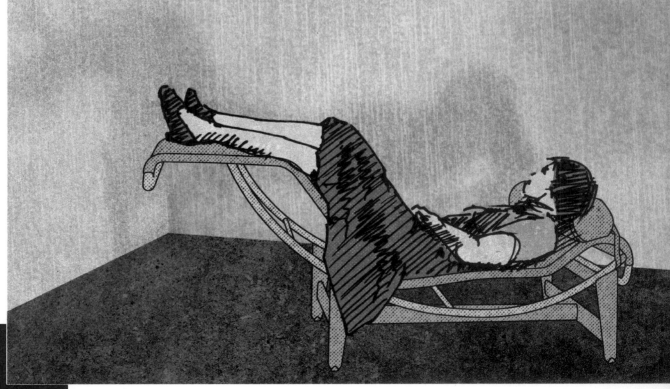

Women, Chairs, Modernism

By Albert Fuster

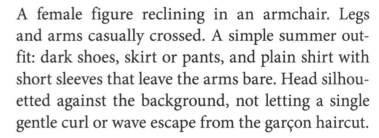

A female figure reclining in an armchair. Legs and arms casually crossed. A simple summer outfit: dark shoes, skirt or pants, and plain shirt with short sleeves that leave the arms bare. Head silhouetted against the background, not letting a single gentle curl or wave escape from the garçon haircut.

The woman's figure triples, now hazy and blurred, now foreshortened, casting a bold shadow on the smooth wall, now covered by a hard, unsettling metal mask. Her clear, solid, and even eerie presence is conditioned by little tricks, photographic devices, dramatic technical effects with social and cultural impact.

Little by little, their identities emerge in contrast to the chairs that cradle them. They are Aino Aalto, photographed in the 1930s in the armchair she and her husband Alvar designed for the Paimio sanatorium; Charlotte Perriand, lying on the chaise longue she designed with Le Corbusier in a magical snapshot taken around 1929; and a young student posing with a mask designed by Oskar Schlemmer in Marcel Breuer's chair, photographed at the Bauhaus in 1927.

These three images, associated with three of the most iconic chairs of the modern era, are gut-wrenching. Three women emerge from the shadows of anonymity, testing the limits of a convention that forces them to submit, both physically and conceptually, to the rigors of a visual code. The resulting images reveal a determination to tear the thin curtain that divides the creating subject from the created object. And they construct a fundamental, though not yet victorious, landscape in the quest for a room of one's own in the world of modern design.

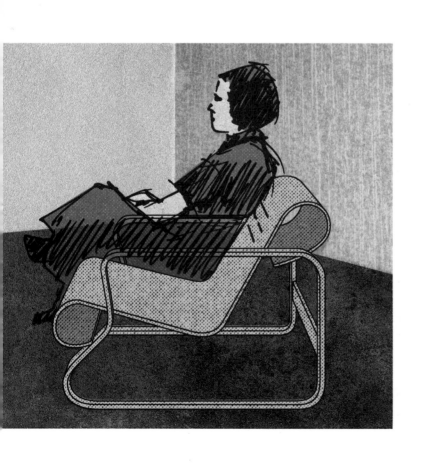

Inadvertent Symbol of a Design Philosophy

By Isabel del Río

The ambitious plan was taking shape, slowly but steadily. The new school was under construction on the Kuhberg, a hill in Baden-Württemberg, just as he had envisioned. A great campus, complete with classrooms, workshops, library, student residence hall, housing for professors, offices for department heads, and even a cafeteria.

The Hochschule für Gestaltung (HfG) in Ulm had been designed in 1950 based on the criteria of functionality and austerity, as the architect, Swiss designer Max Bill, had studied at the Bauhaus Dessau. In April 1953 he was appointed director of the school and head of the Architecture and Urban Planning Department, as he had hoped and wished, having actively participating in the process of designing the curriculum and hiring international teachers. Classes commenced in August of that year, but they had to use an old building as the new premises were not yet finished.

Despite its intention of operating as a private school, unlike the Bauhaus, the HfG relied on annual subsidies from the German federal government and public funding provided by Baden-Württemberg and Ulm City Council. These financial limitations posed a problem, because the temporary classrooms and student and teacher housing facilities were in urgent need of furniture. Max Bill thought of Hans Gugelot, an architect and furniture designer who later became head of the Product Design Department. And they hit upon the solution: they would make their own chairs in the woodworking shops, using donated planks and the skilled hands of master carpenter Paul Hildinger.

The result was the first tangible object to emerge from that school: a backless chair—a stool—whose frame was based on a simple, lightweight cube. This humble piece of furniture consisted of three spruce wood planks connected by dovetail joints. A round beech crossbar braced the bottom of the stool, providing stability as well as a footrest. The clever invention worked, and nearly one hundred copies were made.

The stools were everywhere on campus: the cafeteria, the classrooms, the courtyard, and even the students' rooms. The crossbar made them easy to pick up and carry from one class to the next. The stool was also quite versatile: it could be used as a seat, side table, shelf, desk, etc. The school's new campus was finally inaugurated in October 1955. By that time, the facilities were already well-stocked with these democratic stools, for everyone—students and professors alike—had come to see them as the symbol of something greater, an ethical and aesthetic philosophy of design.

Bardi's Bowl

By Albert Fuster

Lina Bo Bardi took a fresh, cheerful, sensual approach to design, using colors, shapes, and unlikely associations. To a certain extent, hers was a subversive vision, derived from the habitual means by which modern art and architecture have always sought to renew themselves: childlike naivety, primitive or precolonial cultures, unconventional outsider perspectives. But unlike other examples of postwar design, in Bo Bardi's work everything rang true. Her approach was neither superficial nor opportunistic. She was genuinely determined to subvert the dominant trend in industrial design (male, European, capitalist) by practicing a brand of honest design, one that engaged with people and especially with the country that became her home in the 1950s.

The Bardi's Bowl chair can be seen as a compromise between the powerful influence of modern European furniture—with its precise, domineering metal tubes, formal clarity, and universal appeal—and the latent Brazilian world, a patchwork based on fracture and bold, unexpected combinations of materials, colors, and forms. The chair grew from the same seed as the insect figurine the designer fashioned from a burnt-out light bulb, or the toys and objects designed by Brazilian citizens which Bo Bardi included in many of her exhibitions to prove that design exists outside the professional world and the consumer markets: formal, functional, aesthetic designs typical of a "pre-artisanal" world.

With this simple armchair, Bo Bardi paved the way for a new concept of design which, despite originating on the fringes of mainstream culture, needs not play a secondary role. In the forms, materials, and colors of Brazil's culture, people, and territory, the designer found inspiration for a new brand of design, a renewal of the discipline, as well as a solid foundation on which to build a new society.

Sitting on Air

By Mónica Piera

In the world of portable furniture, Gio Ponti's Superleggera is the perfect seat. Light in weight and appearance but structurally solid, the concept is derived from the side chairs, also called lightweight designs, that different European cities began mass-producing in the late eighteenth century. The Chiavari chair in Italy, the Vitoria in Spain, and the Marseille in France are the ancestors of the 1957 Superleggera.

Those earlier models furnished middle-class homes, but above all they were used at street performances and theaters, rented on the boulevards in big cities, and carried to Sunday mass. They were the ultimate portable chairs. The seat was always made of plant fibers, and the wooden frame consisted of plain turned posts and flat slats with mortise-and-tenon joints. The wood might be untreated, stained to imitate more costly species, or decorated with fashionable scenes, often printed.

Ponti studied those models carefully before turning lightweight seating for the masses into an exclusive chair for prosperous interiors. He cleverly transformed structural simplicity into beauty and lightweight practicality into elegance. To this end, he replaced cheap wood with ever-hardy ash, minimized the structural elements, refined the forms, and enlarged the voids until he had reduced the chair to its most basic essence, a chair that almost feels like sitting on air.

Anything Can Happen

By Albert Fuster

Certain combinations seem virtually impossible nowadays. Aldo Rossi had a rare combination of boundless cultural experience, strong political convictions, and a poetic vision of the world. In his wonderful *Scientific Autobiography*, these three elements are constantly intertwined, weaving a cultural document of incalculable literary and architectural value and proving that, as Adolf Loos (whom Rossi greatly admired) claimed, the best architects are also great writers.

Rossi saw the design process as a moral commitment to one's time and context. In design, whether it's an urban layout, a building, or a chair, the designer's duty is to ensure that the tension between physical setting, imagination, and future vision moves in the best possible direction. This position denotes a vision of the creative process in which the individual's conscious actions seem to harmonize with forces greater than him/herself, material, the passage of time...

Rossi summed up the power of this concept of the creative process in a few lines: "In the act of buying an old piece of furniture, we almost find the measure, the comparison with an unknown person, just as taking up a new piece of furniture is practically a resolve to chart our own future. These ideas sound strange, but when I design a piece of furniture, I always recall that odd piece of wood which could have become furniture but instead ended up being a puppet that finally turned into Pinocchio. It was certainly a fantastic piece of wood, but it's not impossible for such things to happen."

A chair like the Milano is a piece of wood, casually transformed by design, but with the potential to produce an entire universe. Who knows? Anything can happen.

The First Chair

By Rosalía Torrent

Today I got a short lesson in physics. An impromptu teacher reminded me of something as basic as the composition of an atom. In the center, he explained, is the nucleus, made up of protons and neutrons. Electrons encircle the nucleus, orbiting around it but prudently keeping their distance. There's nothing between them and the nucleus except empty space.

Everything is made up of atoms; ergo, everything is made up of empty space. This explains the dominance of the void in the First chair, with a back inspired by the atomic nucleus and arms that represent spinning electrons. The riotous postmodernism that spawned it, filtered through the mind and hand of Michele De Lucchi, could not combine shapes and colors in this case. Instead, it held back, teetering on the very brink of the abyss that flooded the 1980s with overwhelming proposals. As a result, the First even became quite popular, as it was symbolic enough to satisfy the exegetes of the new era, but also understated enough that it didn't run the risk of over-dazzling a room. And, as mentioned, it capitalized on vacancy. Opportunity came knocking for De Lucchi when Ettore Sottsass, impressed by the young architect's potential, invited him to join the Memphis group, and this chair ended up being one of their first big hits.

Maybe he was reminded of the First when, years later, the power company came knocking—this time literally. In 2001, Enel hired the Italian architect and designer to create a new smart electricity meter, the second generation of which appeared in 2016. With its almost stylistic smoothness and neutral color, it attests to the versatility of an artist who has produced some of the most coveted interiors in international design, as well as (electricity again) the perfect Tolomeo, a minimal lamp with maximum functionality.

But let's get back to the First. The disc that serves as the back (the atom's nucleus) is the color of the sky, the same hue traditionally used to represent noble gases. The armrests defy convention and turn black. The rest is steely gray. And then there's the open space, nothingness, the power of transparency. A circle only completed in our minds by the law of closure contains an atom, taken out of context and astonished at the new mission it has been given. Circular seat. Legs with identical sections. Understatement. If it weren't a contradiction in terms, we might call it postmodern minimalism. Or perhaps, to save face and furniture, we could say the chair is a paradox.

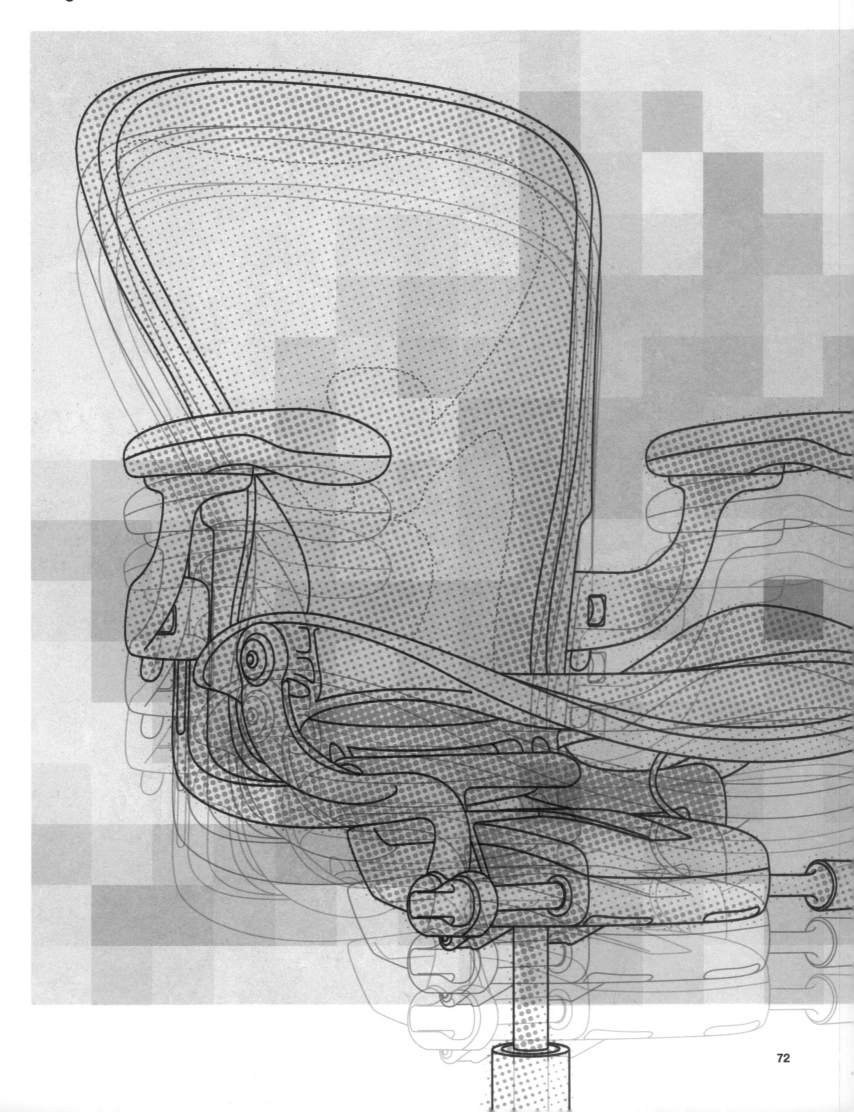

Final Project

By Daniel Giralt-Miracle

At Instituto Gestalt, a school focused on the technological and engineering aspects of design, university students were assigned a final project where they had to determine which chair, in their opinion, best served the needs of the user from an anatomical, functional, technical, and economic perspective. It turned out to be quite a challenge for the young disciples, who wanted to review the most important designs created since 1914—in other words, after the point when functionality, rationalism, and industrialization definitively overcame the primacy of Art Nouveau forms. They pored over the literature on seating furniture in Eastern and Western cultures and eventually narrowed their focus to pieces designed by legends like Eero Saarinen, Marcel Breuer, Gerrit Rietveld, Arne Jacobsen, Charles and Ray Eames, the Antonio Bonet Castellana trio, Juan Kurchan, and Jorge Ferrari. And they didn't just study these chairs theoretically; they found ways to try and test them. Even so, they couldn't decide which to pick as their "ideal chair," given the wide range of opinions and criteria by which they were judging the models.

A consensus was finally reached with the Aeron chair, designed in 1994 by Don Chadwick and Bill Stumpf. The students concluded that this was the chair that best summed up the spirit of our age, with the best combination of ergonomics, mobility, and comfort thanks to the intelligent use of new technology. News of their project reached the ears of the Aeron's creators, who were so flattered that they invited the students to visit their workshop for a personal explanation of their working method and the design process they had followed with this model, as well as their relationship with industrialists. They even persuaded the manufacturer to get involved in the initiative, and so a group of kids from Barcelona ended up traveling to the United States for an experience which, in addition to being unforgettable, made an excellent addition to their resumes that would prove very useful in future job searches.

Design Classics

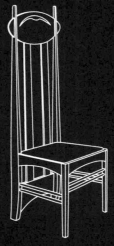

The No. 14 chair designed by Michael Thonet brought furniture into the Industrial Age. It is made by bending wood with steam (bentwood) and consists of just six pieces, ten screws, and two nuts. It has been manufactured by Gebrüder Thonet since 1859. —*Page 49*

Charles Rennie Mackintosh (1868–1928) put Scotland on the map of artistic decoration thanks to the unique personality of his architecture, interior design, and exquisitely crafted furniture. Among his most famous creations are his chairs with high, narrow backs. The first was designed in 1898 for the Argyle Tearoom, and they are still manufactured today as part of Cassina's "I Maestri" collection. —*Page 51*

Gerrit Thomas Rietveld (1888–1964) designed and built the "antecessor" chair for the gatehouse of the Dutch castle of Zuylen in 1906, when he was still an apprentice in his father's cabinetmaking workshop. A few years down the road, in 1918, he added red and blue paint to his most famous design, and after joining the De Stijl movement in 1924 he rechristened it the Red Blue chair. One decade later, he designed the Zig-Zag chair, which has become another classic in the history of design. Both pieces are in the catalogue of the Italian firm Cassina. —*Page 53*

The 1006 Navy chair was invented in 1944 in response to a commission to furnish submarines. The contract apparently specified that the chair had to be strong enough to survive a torpedo blast. It is manufactured in Pennsylvania by Emeco (Electric Machine and Equipment Company) and, like the original, is still made of aluminum. In 2010, the company introduced a recycled plastic version called the 111 Navy, made of 111 PET bottles and created in partnership with Coca-Cola. Recently it also began manufacturing the chair in wood, with the same organic forms as the original model, which over the years has become a genuine design classic. —*Page 57*

Charles and Ray Eames married in 1941, and the chairs they designed together would fill many pages of this *Chairpedia*. They made chairs of molded plywood, like the LCW (1945), as well as plastic shell seats, such as the DAR with its Eiffel base (1950), and chairs with cast aluminum frames, like the EA 105 (1958) from the Aluminum Chairs series. As new technologies were invented, the Eameses evolved with them. Charles passed away in 1978, and his wife Ray died ten years later, in 1988. Their designs are manufactured by the American firm Herman Miller. In 1957, Vitra was licensed to produce and distribute them in Europe and the Middle East. —*Page 55*

Harry Bertoia (1915–1978) was an Italian-born artist who immigrated to the United States to become a modern furniture designer. He studied painting and learned how to work metal, a skill that came in handy when Hans and Florence Knoll invited him to design a collection for Knoll, which included the Bertoia Diamond and Bertoia Side Chair. They went on the market in 1952 and became eternal design legends thanks to their sculptural wire seats. They sold so well that Bertoia was able to do what he loved best and become a full-time sound sculptor. —*Page 59*

1,850 grams of wood and wicker were all that Grandpa Ponti needed to make a good chair. Designers of the world, clench your buttocks! That's what Fernando Amat of Vinçon fame replied when someone asked him what his favorite chair was. Gio Ponti (1897–1979) was one of the most influential names in Italian design and architecture in the 1950s. He founded *Domus* magazine, the Triennale di Milano, and the Compasso d'Oro Award, among other things. One of his best-known architectural creations is the Pirelli Tower in Milan. He began designing it around 1951, at the same time as the Superleggera. Cassina put his chair into production in 1957. —*Page 67*

Aldo Rossi (1931–1997) was an architect and a trendsetter, in theory and in practice. His drawings have the same personality as his architectural plans for works like the Teatro del Mundo, a floating theater with a seating capacity of 250 built for the 1979 Venice Biennale. In 1987, he designed the Milano chair for the Italian firm Molteni&C. In 1990 he was awarded the Pritzker Prize. —*Page 69*

The Memphis group was a collective founded in 1980 by Ettore Sottsass in collusion with other colleagues, who shared a keen desire to experiment with unexpected forms and extravagant colors, break with the status quo, and move away from functionalist design. They changed the motto "form follows function" to "form follows fun." One of its founders was Michele De Lucchi, who in addition to contributing intellectual creativity, designed several pieces for the group's furniture collection, compiled in the Memphis Milano catalogue. The First chair, designed in 1983, fulfilled all the Memphis tenets and was an unexpected commercial success. —*Page 71*

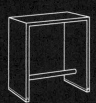

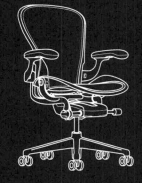

Max Bill studied at the Bauhaus and was the first director of the prestigious Hochschule für Gestaltung, better known as the Ulm School of Design, founded by a motley group of teachers who made design history in their respective fields: painter and theoretician Tomás Maldonado, graphic designer and typographer Otl Aicher, architect and industrial designer Hans Gugelot, and many others. The stool they invented in 1954 became a symbol of their progressive spirit and a shining example of a design philosophy in which form follows function. —*Page 63*

Lina Bo Bardi (1914–1992) studied architecture in Rome, where she was born, and worked with Gio Ponti in Milan before moving to Brazil after World War II, where she spent most of her professional career as an architect, designer, set designer, illustrator, and editor. She designed the Bardi's Bowl chair in 1951, the same year she drew up the plans for the Casa de Vidro, one of her most famous creations and now home to the Instituto Bardi. In 2013 Arper, in collaboration with the institute, produced a limited edition (500 units) of the armchair in its original black leather version. —*Page 65*

The Aeron chair was designed by Donald Chadwick and William Stumpf (1936–2006) in 1994 for Herman Miller, an American company specialized in office furniture.

Prior to his partnership with Chadwick, Stumpf had created the Ergon chair in 1976 after he spent ten years studying how people sit when they work and how their sitting postures affected them. This design is considered the first ergonomic office chair. —*Page 73*

Homar's Chair

By Daniel Giralt-Miracle

In the twentieth century, the most admired zone in Barcelona was the Quadrat d'Or or "Golden Square," in the heart of the Eixample district designed by engineer Ildefons Cerdà, where wealthy Catalan families decided to take up residence, promoting the construction of singular buildings at the height of the Catalan Modernist movement. The Boixareu family, who owned some of the many textile factories that flourished during World War I, decided to take over the main floor of one of those buildings and redecorate it in the *Modernista* style, sparing no expense. They hired Gaspar Homar, one of the most reputable furniture makers of the day, to furnish their dining room. In addition to the dining table and chairs, he made a pair of side tables, several side chairs, a buffet table, and a sideboard. Yet of all the pieces he created, the family's favorite was a simple side chair because, although its structure was that of a conventional chair with a velvet upholstered seat, Homar customized it with exquisite inlays of Japanese-style floral motifs on the back, apron, and legs.

However, the Boixareu family's attachment to their furniture faded over the years, and when the third generation of heirs took possession of the apartment, they decided to replace those furnishings with more modern, functional pieces and called in a secondhand dealer, who cleared out the apartment for a song. What they didn't know was that the astute junkman had found a treasure trove which he peddled to different antique dealers. He sold the pieces separately at a significant profit, and they ended up in shop windows, antique fairs, and international antiquarian shows, until one day a curator from the Musée d'Orsay spied that side chair, realized its worth, and decided to acquire it for the museum's collection, where it still sits today. And so, thanks to a historic twist of fate, Homar, who was born in Mallorca and died in Barcelona, is now renowned and admired as one of the greatest designers of international modernism.

Gaudí and Personalized Ergonomics

By Santi Barjau

Antoni Gaudí's architecture has tremendous international appeal, as the residents of Barcelona know all too well. But in addition to buildings, this artist also created remarkable domestic furniture, designing pieces tailor-made for each client. The most noteworthy are undoubtedly his organic, warm, highly original chairs.

Gaudí designed seats for some of his most important clients, including Calvet, Batlló, and Milà. There's a story about one of these chairs which, like so many other things in Gaudí's life, has spawned many versions, doubts, and controversies. Gaudí was quite a celebrity even in his own lifetime, and so much was said about him that it's often hard to tell which parts of those reports are true. In fact, most of the quotes attributed to Gaudí were transmitted orally and are therefore not entirely reliable.

Some sources say that, on one occasion, Gaudí designed a custom chair for a female client by having her sit on a lump of fresh plaster, which gave him a negative mold of her buttocks that he could use to define the form of the wooden chair: if true, this would be one of the first instances of personalized ergonomics. Unfortunately, another version of the same anecdote has survived, this one featuring a male model: Gaudí supposedly made the chairs for Casa Milà from a cast of the backside of bricklayer who was working on the house. Is this a recurring design strategy? An apocryphal tale with different twists? Or a true story that scholars just haven't been able to fully corroborate?

The anecdote made its way into John Alaimo's docudrama *Antonio Gaudí: The Unfinished Vision* (1974), where Spanish actor José Luis López Vázquez played the famous architect: in one scene, the carpenter can't figure out how to shape the chair, and Gaudí gives him an empirical demonstration. While we can neither confirm nor deny the veracity of either version, it is interesting to note that, apparently, Gaudí had tried to design different furniture for men and women at one point, but the lady of the house flatly rejected the idea.

The Story of a Survivor

By María José Balcells

Transforming La Pedrera, Gaudí's legendary building, was quite a daunting prospect. Some felt it was a sacrilege, while others applauded the idea. The tricky task fell to the Catalan architect Francisco J. Barba Corsini, a man of frail appearance but firm resolve and, most importantly, respectful of his colleagues and clients.

Even before I knew that it had greatly influenced him, I always associated Barba Corsini with King Vidor's film *The Fountainhead*, based on the Ayn Rand novel which they say was inspired by Frank Lloyd Wright's life. When I watched the final scene where Gary Cooper stands, arms akimbo, atop his building, I always imagined Barba Corsini doing the same on the rooftop of La Pedrera. That pose wasn't an act of hubris but of meditative contemplation.

In 1953, Barba Corsini was hired to remodel the attic level—abandoned because it was deemed useless—of Gaudí's building. The goal was to eliminate the existing laundry and storage facilities and create *apartamientos*, as the press called them at the time. He worked on site for two years to complete the job. In addition to the interiors, Barba Corsini also designed all the furnishings, as the stylish furniture available on the market at the time was not aesthetically suited to the unique setting of La Pedrera. Looking at his drawings, I think that he may been inspired by cartoons as well as movies. The colors, shapes, and materials in his sketches conjure up images of the Flintstones living in them. But when I observe the magnificent black-and-white photographs taken by Francesc Català-Roca, the interiors and their furnishings exude a simple, extremely modern air, probably owing to the fact that the tenants included intellectuals, artists, and a considerable number of foreigners.

One of the furniture pieces Barba Corsini designed in 1955 is the dining room chair, a simple seat created specifically for its intended setting and space. The shape, reminiscent of the parabolic arches in the apartments, and the choice of materials—calibrated steel tubes for the legs and hardboard for the shell—gave it a look that went perfectly with the new architecture.

The outline of the seat and back, made in one piece and based on a cardboard model, recalls certain American and European chairs from the 1950s, which Barba Corsini had seen in architecture magazines, films, and his travels. Hardboard was also an inexpensive material that could be finished in a wide variety of colors to make a nice contrast with the black flooring in the apartments.

The lofts were dismantled in 1995 to leave the attic space as Gaudí had originally designed it. The architect and gallerist Joaquim Ruiz Millet rescued some of the furniture, and thanks to him this chair, of which approximately one hundred units were produced, has been given a second lease on life in a new edition made using more contemporary materials to facilitate mass production.

Torres Clavé's Cadirat

By Rosalía Torrent

In the final hours of his life, haunted by the fear of falling into Nazi hands, philosopher Walter Benjamin may have reminisced about the warm afternoons he spent on the island of Ibiza. Perhaps he relived the pleasant, familiar sensation of houses with gleaming white walls and interiors glimpsed through open doors (his own words), furnished with strikingly beautiful wickerwork chairs whose true secret was the sobriety, the austerity of their presence in that space. At Portbou, the Spanish town on the border with France where Benjamin spent those final hours, Franco's new police force had blocked his flight to freedom. He took an overdose of morphine. It was September 1940.

If the trenches that architect and designer Josep Torres Clavé had been digging one year earlier had managed to repel Franco's nationalist forces in the Spanish Civil War, the German philosopher would have had no trouble crossing the border. But the trenches failed to stop the rebels and instead became Torres Clavé's grave when they were attacked by Italian bombers. In his last moments, perhaps he also briefly flashed back to Ibiza, the island that inspired his Cadirat, a beautifully woven chair which had shared the same space as Picasso's Guernica and Calder's *Mercury Fountain* at the 1937 Exposition Internationale in Paris. Old black-and-white photos of the Spanish Republican Pavilion show dozens of these armchairs, lined up together like a miniature army of peace and repose.

Just a few years before the untimely deaths of Benjamin and Torres Clavé, in the early 1930s, Ibiza had become a magical haven for artists and writers. Its quiet streets and landscapes may not have cured Dadaists Tristan Tzara and Raoul Hausmann of their nihilism or alleviated Cioran's pessimism, but the island certainly inspired members of the Group of Catalan Architects and Experts for the Advancement of Contemporary Architecture (GATCPAC), including the designer of this armchair. Both Torres Clavé and his colleague Josep Lluís Sert were actively involved in organizational disputes.

Like other architects of their generation, they felt that the Modern Movement had gone a bit overboard with steel and chrome and believed it was time for a change. On Ibiza, they saw houses and traditional furniture which seemed to embody the kind of comfort that movement aspired to achieve, but also the warmth required for essential human intimacy. And so this chair was born, a reassuringly familiar form with all the confidence of an object that stands the test of time, with the robustness of its oak frame, with those reinforcing stretchers, and with the woven rope that reminds us of human labor and handiwork.

Mies with a Twist

By María José Balcells

Probably no one knows that this rocking chair owes its existence to an extravagant piece of furniture called the Arcada. It was part of the "First Special Furniture Collection," and thanks to Fernando Amat, the well-connected owner of Vinçon, in 1979 the catalogue of that collection made its way into the hands of Gilles de Bure, the art and design critic and curator, and Jeffrey Osborne, Vice President of Design at Knoll International. The Arcada made such an impression that Knoll invited Carles Riart to participate in their Progression program to commemorate the 50th anniversary of Mies van der Rohe's Barcelona Chair, which the New York-based company had been producing since 1947.

Riart was commissioned to design a chair that had the same simple forms and solid presence as Mies's masterpiece. It was quite a daunting prospect, not only because it involved revisiting an icon of modernism made by a legendary architect, but also because of the tight schedule (the chair had to be market-ready in six months) and because the other nine participants in the program were world-renowned architects and designers like Robert Venturi and Richard Meier, who moreover had been working on the project for some time already.

But if there's one thing that stimulates Riart's creativity, it's a good challenge. He soon decided that his design should be both popular and exquisite, American like the company that would produce it yet infused with Mies's Old World refinement. American Shakers, Viennese workshops, and the Bauhaus swirled together in his brain, forming a potent cocktail, and the result was the Riart Rocker, which combined a popular American typology with visibly fine craftsmanship and formal and technological modernity.

After three intense months of thinking and drawing, with the expert assistance of Muebles Casas, Riart made three different prototypes, all extremely sober and elegant yet also bold and suggestive. The carefully packed chairs arrived in Manhattan, and when the crates were opened everyone present unanimously burst into applause. All three chairs, one in white wood and the other two also made of wood but stained deep red and navy blue, had a dramatic presence. The model finally put into production was an innovative twist on the Barcelona chair: Riart had switched from an elitist typology to a democratic one, from steel to wood, and from rationalism to the crime of ornament, all without sacrificing one iota of modernism.

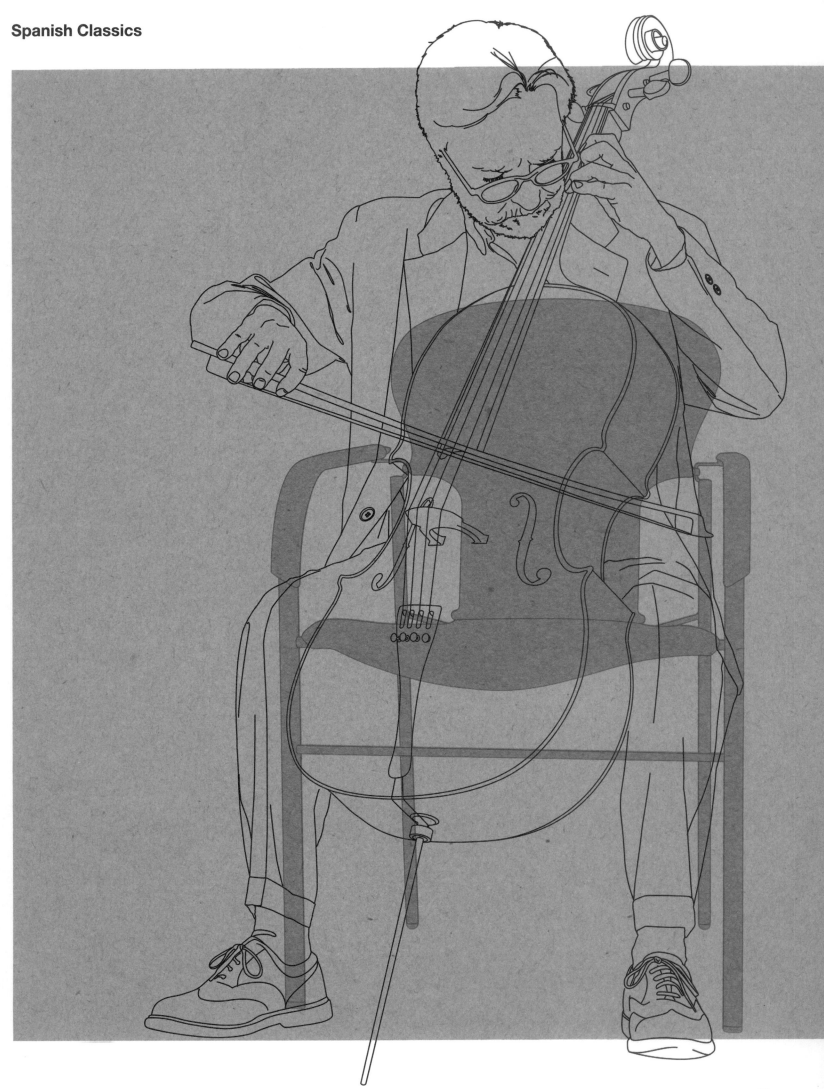

A Refined Popular Classic

By María José Balcells

An expectant hush descends as Anne-Sophie Mutter and her Lord Dunn-Raven appear on the stage of the Palau de la Música in Barcelona. Tchaikovsky's violin concerto begins and the first notes waft from the strings of an instrument so famous it has its own name, an object of great beauty and delicacy with a special sound that makes it unique. This Stradivarius from 1710 may well be one of the most extraordinary violins ever made.

In that privileged setting, the music washes over the audience, but many of them have no idea that the chairs they're sitting in were inspired by that magical instrument. The design is called Varius because its seat and back imitate the silhouette of the famous violins and cellos crafted by master luthier Antonio Stradivari. The chair's delicate, attractive curves invite you to sink into them: like the melodies emanating from that remarkable violin, it envelops you in ergonomic comfort and elegance.

The Varius started out as an armchair designed by the architect Oscar Tusquets in 1983 for the Casas firm. It is quite versatile, with different versions for private residences, offices, and public spaces. It's also stackable, though at first glance you wouldn't think so, and that space-saving option makes it more competitive. But the Varius wasn't an only child; it entered the world accompanied by a version on casters, a high stool with a footrest, an executive armchair, a seat for public venues, and even a rocker called the Bavarius.

In 1984 it was shortlisted for the Delta Awards of the ADI-FAD (Association of Industrial Designers, Promotion of the Decorative Arts) and won the Critics' Award, granted not by a panel of experts but by the public—the Varius was already becoming a popular chair. By the end of that decade it was a best seller, and its success helped Casas become the first company to win the National Design Prize, a distinction likewise granted to Tusquets in 1988. The chair sold well and was constantly in demand, and when Casas closed in 2003, a pioneering Spanish firm called BD Barcelona Design took over its production.

After more than thirty years on the market, the Varius is a refined popular classic that has posed with all sorts of prominent people, from design historian Gillo Dorfles and media personality Boris Izaguirre to photographer Ouka Leele, architect Beth Galí, and Dr. Santiago Dexeus, to name but a few. Another illustrious user is the artist Antonio López, who trimmed the legs of the Varius in his studio. "It's just that María and I are both so short...." Art cut down to size.

The Andrea Challenge

By María José Balcells

"Touché!" the fencer shouts, and the two opponents lower their foils. With *verdadera destreza* or true skill (as the first Spanish fencing treatise, published in 1472, defined this art), Josep Lluscà used foils as the inspiration for the Andrea chair's legs. In addition to fencing, this project had two other points of reference, Mr. and Mrs. Eames and Antoni Gaudí: the former because, in the 1940s, they tried to create a three-legged plywood chair, but the design was never produced because it lacked stability; and the latter because Lluscà was fascinated by the chair Gaudí designed for Casa Calvet (ca. 1902), made entirely of wood. With these two seats in mind, Lluscà set himself a challenge: he would create a commercially viable, stable, three-legged chair as sturdy as Gaudí's design. He labored long and hard over his project, doing research and studying centers of gravity to achieve the greatest possible degree of stability, and evaluating all production possibilities.

Andrea is made of steel, aluminum, and solid beech wood. The elliptical curve of the back embraces the sitter, and the rounded edges of the arms give the aluminum a hint of warmth. Despite its classic, semi-artisanal appearance, it was actually conceived as a blend of technology and tradition: a conventional material like wood carved with CNC machinery (Computer Numerical Control, cutting-edge technology in the 1980s) to facilitate mass production. The result was a comfortable, inviting chair with a "classic modern" look. In 1986 the designer pitched his idea to a company that turned him down. Two years later, Andreu World commissioned him to design a chair that would set the firm apart from its competitors and potentially become an icon of the brand. Lluscà knew exactly what to do: he would create a three-legged chair and name it Andrea in honor of its manufacturer.

Spanish Classics

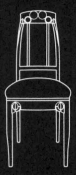

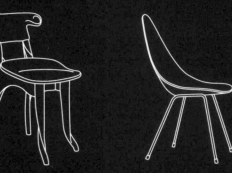

Gaspar Homar (1870–1953) was one of the most prominent figures in the Catalan Modernist decorative arts, a contemporary of other European furniture makers like Hector Guimard and William Morris. He studied at the Llotja School in Barcelona and learned cabinetmaking at the Vidal Workshops. He regularly worked with architects like Josep Puig i Cadafalch and Lluís Domènech i Montaner, and his vast and varied output—including all sorts of wooden furniture pieces, metalwork creations, textiles, and mosaic panels—is now part of the history of interior decoration. —*Page 77*

Antoni Gaudí (1852–1926) is undoubtedly Spain's best-known architect. But that international fame isn't limited to his buildings. His holistic concept of architecture extended to all the decorative aspects of a structure, including furniture. This inspired him to create pieces like the Batlló chair (1906), on which the legend of his client's backside rests, or the iconic Calvet chair (1902), which is actually a solid oak armchair. BD Barcelona Design was the first company to retrieve them from the annals of history in 1978, mass producing them with the same materials used in the originals. —*Page 79*

La Pedrera is the popular name given to Casa Milà, a residential building designed and constructed by Antoni Gaudí in Barcelona between 1906 and 1910. The chair that F. J. Barba Corsini (1916–2008) designed in 1955 for the modern apartments which occupied the building's attic level for some years bears the same name: the Pedrera chair. Joaquim Ruiz Millet and Ana Planella, working under the author's supervision, relaunched it in 1994 via Galería H20. —*Page 81*

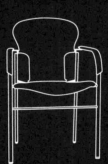

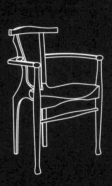

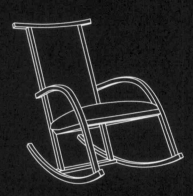

Josep Torres Clavé was born in Barcelona in 1906 and died in the Spanish Civil War in 1939, when a bomb raid hit the trenches he was digging at the front. Five years earlier he had designed this seat, inspired by Ibiza's traditional *cadirat* chairs, to furnish the Spanish Republican Pavilion at the 1937 Exposition Internationale in Paris. It was first sold at the Barcelona shop he had founded with Josep Lluís Sert and Antonio Bonet, called MIDVA (a Catalan acronym standing for Furniture and Decoration for the Modern Home), which they used to promote their rationalist ideas. Today the chair is manufactured by Mobles 114 under the name Torres Clavé 1934. —*Page 83*

Oscar Tusquets designed the Varius for the Casas firm in 1983, and two decades later it was taken on by BD Barcelona Design, which enlarged the family with a new, simpler version christened the Minivarius that went on to become an iconic chair in the contemporary history of Spanish design. Tusquets also created the Gaulino chair, designed in 1987 for Carlos Jané Camacho, another classic that was added to the BD catalogue after the original manufacturer went out of business. —*Page 87*

Carles Riart is a design artisan who co-founded the Gris shop in Barcelona in 1969 with the Spanish film director Bigas Luna. Like all of his creations, the Riart Rocker is a high-quality piece of furniture with a blend of mystery and magic in which no detail has been overlooked: ebony and rosewood frame, Utrecht velvet upholstery, almost imperceptible mother-of-pearl inlays, and perfect ergonomic performance and rocking motion. —*Page 85*

   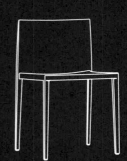 

Josep Lluscà emerged in the 1980s as the ideal prototype of the professional industrial designer: thoughtful, methodical, technically qualified, and commercially profitable. He designed lamps or pressure cookers with equal skill and was one of the first Spanish professionals to work with foreign manufacturers. The launch of his Andrea chair was an aesthetic and commercial success, and to give it a more contemporary, less delicate look better suited to collective use, a second version was created with the seat and back made of polyurethane integral foam. *—Page 89*

William Sawaya began working with Andreu World in 2002, and two years later the Zarina chair (2004) went on the market. Today it remains one of the firm's best sellers in both the home decor and contract furniture sectors. In the 1990s, this architect and designer made a name for himself in Milan, working with his partner Paolo Moroni to establish the Sawaya & Moroni brand. They started out as a design studio and later became a furniture manufacturer, the first that dared to produce the designs of Iranian fellow architect Zaha Hadid.

Piergiorgio Cazzaniga is the son of a cabinetmaker who grew up among woodworkers. Nowadays, only someone with that kind of background could have come up with a chair like the Lake (2018), which would look right at home in his grandparents' house. But he also created the Sail (2012) from gas injection-molded plastic, a chair designed for collective use, crafted with the same skill he brings to woodworking and without an ounce of spare material. And he invented the Flex (2013), more suitable for the workplace. Different purposes, materials, and manufacturing methods, but always united by the common denominators of comfort and durability.

Many Spanish design classics were created by foreign designers. The success of the Seville World's Fair and the Barcelona Olympics in 1992 encouraged many Spanish companies to begin their international expansion. With the dawn of the twenty-first century, the borders of creativity also began to dissolve.

Firms like Andreu World—which up until then had mainly worked with Valencian, Spanish, and naturalized foreign designers like Vicente Soto, Ximo Roca, Ángel Martí, Pedro Miralles, Juan Montesa, Carlos Tíscar, Francis Montesinos, Javier Mariscal, Gabriel Teixidó, Pete Sans, Quod (Esteve Agulló and Mariano Pi), Josep Mora, Gemma Bernal, Ramón Isern, Margarita Viarnés, Jaime Bouzaglo, Santiago Miranda, Josep Lluscà, Nancy Robbins, Jorge Pensi, and Alberto Lievore— started importing talent from abroad. William Sawaya was the first to arrive.

Jasper Morrison is a classic in his own right who needs no introduction. Success came early, almost immediately after opening his London studio, and he designed the Thinking Man's Chair (1988) for Cappellini, the antithesis of the smart minimalist design that has marked the rest of his career. All his work can be described as "super normal"—in other words, simple, functional, and timeless. And practical. For Andreu World, he designed the Unos chair (2016) and, after making barely noticeable technical improvements, quickly replaced it with the Duos (2018).

Patricia Urquiola was born in Spain but trained in Italy. In Milan, where she has lived for more than twenty years, she was taught by Achille Castiglioni and worked with Vico Magistretti and Piero Lissoni before striking out on her own. The first chair she designed for Andreu World, called Nub (2012), sums up the values that define the company: tradition, fine workmanship, and attention to detail. A few years later she created the Nuez chair (2015), an experiment with a thermoplastic shell that embodies two other pillars of the manufacturer's corporate culture: confidence and innovation.

The Monobloc Chair

By Carmen Sevilla

The white plastic chair is the most widely used piece of furniture in the world. I read that and find it mind-boggling. That chair seems invisible to me; perhaps my brain has developed mechanisms that block it out, refusing to acknowledge its virtual omnipresence. But when I stop to think about it, I realize that this chair has supported me on the terrace of my own house for years, withstanding the relentless passage of time; at street concerts, on outdoor movie nights in summer, at sidewalk cafés and restaurants, in the homes of relatives and friends, at protests, lectures and conferences, on the sandy beach, the edge of a cliff, and even in a swimming pool. The list is endless. I've seen it in and out of context. In churches, parades and processions, all sorts of venues. In situations of war and peace. In tiny villages and sprawling metropolises. In the middle of the desert. Dirty, old, and worn. Restored, mended, rebuilt with parts donated by sister chairs. Coveted and prized, chained to lampposts and railings. But also abandoned at dumps and surrounded by rubble.

It's a strong, sturdy, lightweight, useful chair: clean, stackable, comfortable, versatile, and cheap. The epitome of democratic social design: was this what the designers of the early avant-garde movements, the Bauhaus, or Russian Constructivism dreamed of making? Perhaps so, but paradoxically it's been given a bad rap, scorned for its insipid aesthetic presence and rendered suspect by growing ecological awareness.

Martí Guixé requested respect for it in 2009, and other designers have revisited it with consideration, like the Campana brothers and Martino Gamper did for the 2017 exhibition at the Vitra Design Museum. That show, titled *Monobloc — A Chair for the World*, paid tribute to a landmark design: the idea was first mooted in the 1920s, and after several products (like the Panton chair or Vico Magistretti's Selene) came close to hitting the mark, it burst onto the market in the 1970s. Apparently, Henry Massonnet's Fauteuil 300 was the first model to fulfill all the requirements of the Monobloc. This is part of its appeal: despite the chair's popularity and commercial success, it has no pedigree, which may explain why it's been ignored by design purists—and by those of us who didn't think we were.

Here's another mind-boggling thought: how many of these chairs have been made over the years? How many are there today?

The Chair You Can Take Anywhere

By Isabel Campi

Who hasn't headed for the beach or the countryside toting one of those cheap folding aluminum tube chairs? The lawn chair has it all: lightweight, rust-resistant, easy to store, and effortless to carry. But is this campsite fixture a beautiful and comfortable design? Not really.

The curved legs make them wobbly, and if you lean too far to the side they tend to topple over. The metal bar on the back of the seat digs into your buttocks, and the one on the front digs into your thighs, cutting off circulation. The gaps between the interwoven nylon strips widen over time. They're hard to repair, and a strong gust of wind will send them tumbling.

Even so, it's one of the most popular anonymous designs in the world. It appeared on the U.S. market in the 1950s, when the aluminum company Alcoa decided it had to find a profitable use for the tubes it had produced in abundance during World War II.

Despite its poor ergonomics, it turned out to be the right chair at the right time and became indispensable to postwar families determined to live the American dream in the suburbs. No barbecue, yard party, or beach day was complete without the omnipresent lawn chair. And it still isn't today. We even see them in towns and cities on hot summer nights, when people unfold their lawn chairs on the sidewalk and plop down for a leisurely chat with the neighbors.

In the 1950s, Alcoa advertised this model as the chair you can take anywhere; targeting female consumers, the company touted its advantages for housewives, who wouldn't have to wait for their menfolk to carry chairs into the yard anymore.

Over the years, this chair has become a universal model whose prosaic convenience far outweighs its discomfort. It's a chair for practical people who think price and utility are more important than aesthetic appeal, or who own more sophisticated models that allow them to sit comfortably for hours at a time. It may be the chair you can take anywhere, but you won't want to stay there long.

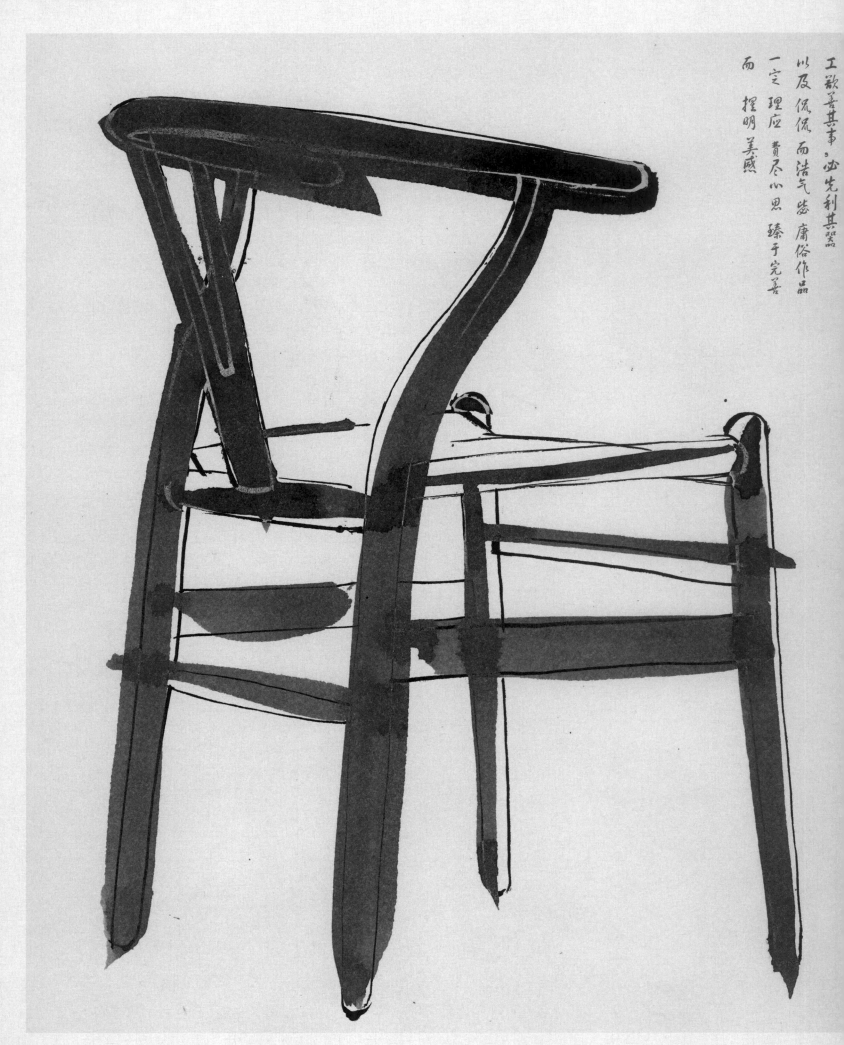

工欲善其事，必先利其器
以及低俗而浮气藐庸俗作品
一定理应 费尽心思 臻于完善
而 擢明 美感

From China to Denmark

By Marisa García Vergara

The Wishbone chair, also called the Y or CH24 chair, designed by Hans J. Wegner in 1949, is an icon of Danish design and, by extension, a hallmark of Scandinavian modernism. Produced continuously since it was first invented, its popularity is rivaled only by Thonet's No. 14 chair. In fact, this rivalry is responsible for its existence: when imports ceased during World War II, Fritz Hansen decided to come up with a design that could replace and compete with Thonet's products. In 1943, he asked Wegner to design a wooden chair using steam-bending technology. However, instead of emulating the simplicity of Thonet's models, Wegner looked to other historical references: the Ming dynasty chairs that had made their way to Denmark thanks to its close trade relations with China.

This style, developed under the influence of Confucian and Taoist philosophies, advocated using the forms of nature as an aesthetic expression of *yuanhun*, a principle that roughly translates as "wholeness" or "roundness," evident in the curving backs that flow into the armrests of these chairs.

So how did a seventeenth-century Chinese chair inspire a modern design icon?

After two years at the furniture design school founded by Kaare Klint in Copenhagen, Wegner had become familiar with Klint's method, based on studying and drawing historical models, and although he later renounced the principles he had been taught, he never lost his love of craftsmanship and reliance on traditional forms. Therefore, it isn't surprising that Wegner thought of *quanyi* chairs and their continuous backs: he knew they could be fashioned from a single piece of bentwood, and the manufacturer had the right equipment to bend pieces of that length. Fritz Hansen produced and sold two of the prototypes he designed. One, a more traditional chair with a leather seat, was manufactured in 1944, and the other, a more modern version with a paper cord seat, appeared in 1945. The latter did not sell well and was soon taken out of production. But Carl Hansen was determined to relaunch it and contacted the designer, and that marked the beginning of a productive partnership which produced some of the most celebrated pieces in Danish design history. In less than three weeks, Wegner came up with four new prototypes for the company, one of which was the CH24, the most refined formal synthesis of this model with a streamlined Y-shaped back that gave the chair its name.

The Wishbone chair has fourteen components, each of which must be individually carved, sanded, and shaped by hand—honoring Master Wegner's love of traditional craftsmanship—before they are assembled. Wegner consistently turned down offers from American companies that wanted to mass-produce his chairs to satisfy the growing demand for organic designs. He believed that his furniture was meant to be crafted by artisans, by hand, and in Denmark. Anything else was unthinkable.

Porset's Miguelito

By Marisa García Vergara

Cuban exile Clara Porset arrived in Mexico with a suitcase full of ideas picked up in the United States and Europe, which she soon mixed with the effervescence of the nationalist movement that sought to revive the traditions and cultural wealth of the Mexican peoples. While studying popular objects, she came across the *butaque*, a cross between the old Spanish X-frame or Savonarola chairs and the pre-Columbian *duhos* that proliferated on the colonial routes of the Manila Galleons. Adapted by native artisans, who incorporated different characteristics and materials in each region, the *butaque* spread to ranches, haciendas, and colonial homes across the Caribbean and eventually reached the United States, where Thomas Jefferson purchased one in 1819 and had it altered and copied.

In the 1930s, when the indigenist euphoria for folk culture and objects was at its peak, designers like William Spratling and Héctor Aguilar came up with their own interpretations of the *butaque*, but it was Clara Porset who studied it thoroughly, tested structural variations to improve its ergonomics, and replaced the seat material, trying a wide variety of fabrics made from different fibers. In the process, she freed the *butaque* from the shackles of tradition and turned it into a modern icon. In 1947 Porset presented it at the Artek-Pascoe showroom in New York, alongside other multipurpose furniture pieces for the modern home. The *butaque* chair stood out from the rest, "clearly betray[ing] its Mexican heritage" according to *The New York Times*.

Combining experimentation with the quest for a distinctive style, one inspired by craftsmanship and tradition yet suited to inexpensive industrial production, Porset's designs shattered conventional notions of indigenous art, offering an image of modernity and progress that fascinated the architects who were determined to build a modern Mexico. The Miguelito armchair, an austere, solid version of the *butaque* with a leather seat and armrests, was designed by Porset for Luis Barragán to furnish his home—built in Tacubaya in 1947—although he didn't always remember to give her credit for it. Porset worked for Mexican intellectuals and businesspeople and helped shape the image of a modernized Mexico, but she never lost her social conscience, and after Fidel Castro's victory in the Sierra Maestra, she went home to Cuba to join the revolutionary cause and design furniture for schools and hospitals. When she returned to Mexico, she stopped receiving commissions from modern Mexican designers and ended up teaching—a stroke of luck for the country's future designers.

Rereading the Past

By Guillem Celada

It wasn't the first time that architects had tried their hand at chair design. Nor was it the first time a chair had served as a prescient miniature model of future architectural solutions.

When the architects Federico Correa and Alfons Milà planned the Reno, a restaurant on Barcelona's legendary Carrer Tuset, they thought of everything from the spatial structure to the furnishings. And they designed a chair which, in hindsight, seems to have foreshadowed the building that would rise on the opposite corner of that very street twenty-five years later.

The Reno chair was a "conceptual scale model," a statement of principles, an aesthetic manifesto. In 1961, its creators presaged the postmodernism that would arrive decades later with a revamped version of a classic Louis xvi armchair in wood and leather upholstery. They repeated this exercise in 1982 when they began to plan the Metro 3 building: a contemporary reworking of historical architecture featuring a facade of Renaissance fantasy and rhythm, synthesized and unified by color and material.

A short time later, they took a similar approach to the building for the Barcelona Provincial Council. Conceived as a backdrop to the Catalan Modernist Casa Serra built by architect Puig i Cadafalch, their design embraced a neo-neoclassicism as the freedom and essence of postmodern shifts.

Their Reno chair had offered a glimpse of this many years earlier, but Correa and Milà's premonitory hint was so subtle that nobody picked up on it. More time would have to pass before Philippe Starck, one of the most celebrated designers of the late twentieth century, proposed the Louis Ghost chair. His rereading of the Louis xvi chair went one step further than our visionaries, reducing it to a piece of transparent plastic: a bold move in a context more conducive to these kinds of plot twists.

Having Your Back—and More

By Pilar Mellado

A dining room usually has a large table with various chairs arranged around it, one for each of the diners, which end up being the center of attention. Dining room sets tend to feature high-backed chairs, a design that reinforces the sensation of a cozy circle of intimacy warmed by the guests sitting around the table and the delicious aromas and steam rising from the hot-cooked dishes. That protected microclimate inspired the shape of Pedro Miralles's Hakernar chair. With this idea in mind, the designer combined the concepts of warmth and comfort with the notion of the chair as a protective shield or piece of armor, like a bodyguard who "has your back."

However, Miralles's creativity didn't end with this back-guard for family gatherings. As on so many other projects, once again his imagination made an intuitive leap and reinvented an archetype. How did he do it? Simple: being the good architect that he was, he turned to the constructed world that had inspired him so often in the past, where he found a simple clay planter and transferred it to the back of his chair. An original or perhaps a bold decision, but undeniably the right one. Moving a common outdoor element to an indoor setting created just the kind of natural microclimate he sought, scenting the air and adding a hint of freshness as only a plant, or plants, can do.

Once upon a time, sitting down to eat as a family or with friends was an everyday occurrence. But the years rolled by, our lifestyle changed, and that tradition is now reserved for holidays or special occasions. That's why designs like this one, which go beyond the object and its aesthetic value, are more meaningful today: every gathering around the table is in itself a cause for celebration that must be protected, cherished, and, above all, enjoyed. May the minutes turn to hours, and may your parting words be to set the date of the next repast.

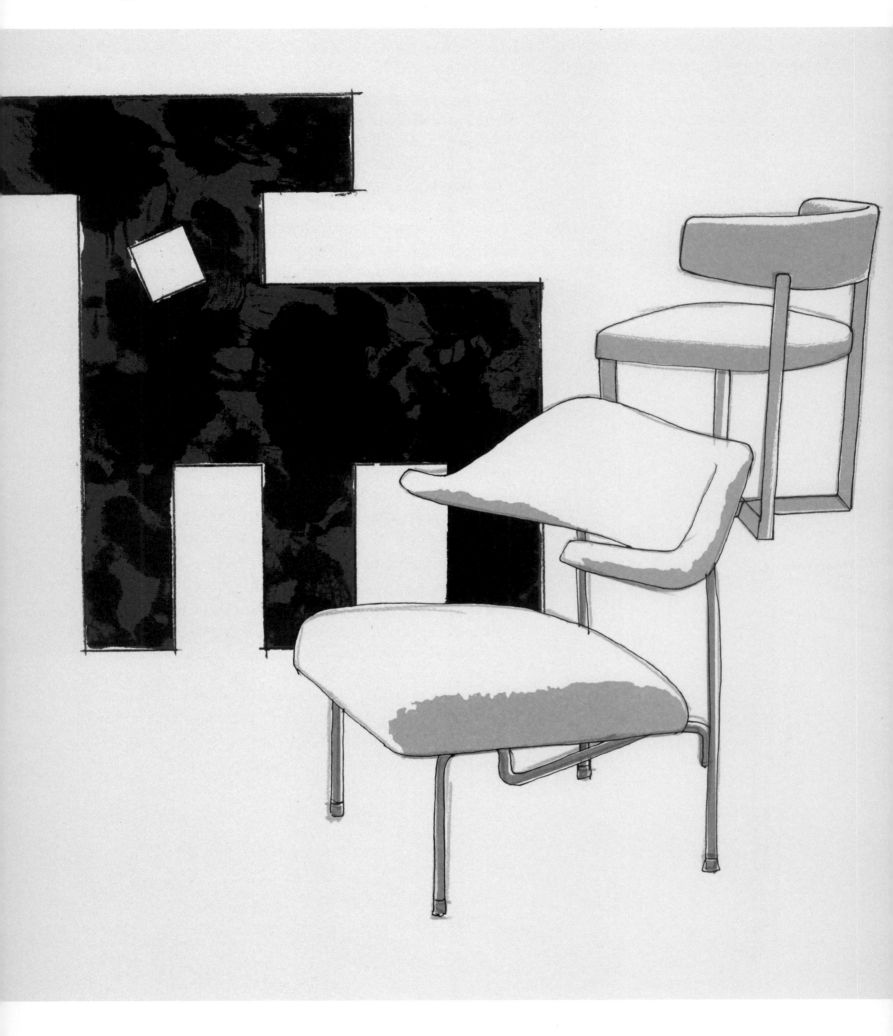

Bullish Airs

By Ana Domínguez

Miguel Fisac was one of those architects who liked to design furniture for his building projects. A globetrotter with an inquiring mind, he steeped himself in Nordic design, which had a strong influence on him; even so, Fisac was always a kind of universal "man of La Mancha," and the legacy of his *manchego* roots permeates his work like a silent yet palpable presence. For proof, we need look no further than his "chicken leg" furniture or his Toro chair and armchair. The latter resembles an updated version of the Castilian friar's chair or *frailera*, an impression reinforced by the back shaped like a bull's nape. But it also strikes us as a chair attuned to modern times, with its separate seat and back, wooden frame, and leather upholstery, a popular choice among Danish designers.

Fisac's armchair—not originally designed for the Spanish firm Darro, though it was eventually added to its catalogue—is a model or archetype that inspired many designers who came after him. A case in point is the Veronica chair designed by Afra and Tobia Scarpa for the Casas firm, which also alludes to the world of bulls: the shape of the back and arms recalls a bullfighting stance known as the *verónica*, when the matador stands before the bull and holds his cape with both hands, waiting for the animal to charge. The Tauro chair by Lievore Altherr Molina for Andreu World, defined by the enveloping curve of its back, also harks back to Fisac's first "bullish" chair.

Archetypes

Hans J. Wegner (1914–2007) designed more than five hundred chairs in his lifetime. Carl Hansen & Son still manufacture two of the most famous models, both designed in 1949: the Round chair and the CH24 or Y chair, also popularly known as "The Chair," in continuous production since 1950. More than one hundred steps are required to manufacture each chair, most of which are carried out by hand. The underside of the seat always has a label or stamp of authenticity. Like many design classics, this piece has inspired countless copies and knockoffs. The best defense against them is still quality. *—Page 97*

The French engineer and businessman Henry Massonnet designed the Fauteuil 300 in 1972, considered the archetype of the cheap one-piece white plastic chair. At the time, he managed to produce one every two minutes. There are many anonymous versions of the Monobloc chair, and no one knows how many are scattered around the world today. *—Page 93*

Alcoa stands for Aluminum Company of America, founded in 1888 and now one of the world's three leading aluminum manufacturers. After inventing aluminum foil in 1910, it came up with other domestic uses for this material, such as the folding lawn chair with an aluminum tube frame, first sold in 1954. This popular model has since become universal and can be purchased online today for less than 20 dollars. *—Page 95*

The shape of the Toro armchair that Miguel Fisac (1913–2006) added to the catalogue of the Madrid firm Darro in the 1950s is as unmistakable and impressive as the one Afra and Tobia Scarpa chose for their Veronica chair. And just in case anyone failed to pick up on the "bullish" reference, the two Italian architects drove their point home by upholstering the entire chair in red and black leather. The Veronica was an icon of Spanish design in the 1980s, produced by the Casas firm, which closed in 2003.

The Tauro chair that Lievore Altherr Molina designed for Andreu World also has a powerful presence and the same formal significance: a contemporary reinterpretation of an ancient symbol. It charged onto the market in 2008 with the same energy as its predecessors. *—Page 105*

The engineer Alberto Meda created the Light Light chair (1987) for Alias. Although his design doesn't intentionally imitate the bull, it still has a strong formal affinity with the archetype. It was an experimental attempt to make a chair as light and durable as possible using aerospace-grade technology and materials which, contrary to what we might think, actually require painstaking manual labor. It's basically a Nomex honeycomb core covered in thin layers of carbon fiber. Meda soared to the outer limits of the possible, but exorbitant manufacturing costs brought him back down to earth. Only a handful of units were sold.

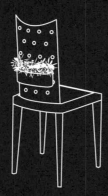

Clara Porset Dumás was born into a well-to-do Cuban family in 1895. She was educated in the United States and Europe, studying at the Columbia University School of the Arts, the École des Beaux-Arts in Paris, and the Bauhausian Black Mountain College, then directed by Josef Albers. When she returned to Cuba, she was an expert in functionalist design. In later life she taught Industrial Design at the Architecture School of the National Autonomous University of Mexico, to which she bequeathed her possessions and her archive when she died in 1981. —*Page 99*

Pedro Miralles was born on August 26, 1955, in Valencia, Spain. An architect by training and designer by vocation, his professional career was short but intense. He died unexpectedly in his hometown on August 30, 1993, just days after his thirty-eighth birthday, leaving a legacy of pieces with a distinctive style that reflected his strong personality. One of them is the Hakernar chair, designed in 1987 for the catalogue of Sedie & Company and commissioned by Massimo Morozzi, who was looking for fresh young talent at the time and was always open to groundbreaking ideas.

Morozzi enthusiastically hailed Miralles's clever idea of using the large surface area of high-backed chairs to support planters: a colorful, flowery touch, like something straight out of an Almodóvar film (Miralles had worked as an extra for the flamboyant director during the Madrid Movida). It was his first job for an international firm—quite an achievement, as such opportunities were rare for Spanish designers at the time, despite the creative exuberance that had begun to sweep across Spain. The name Hakernar comes from Achernar, the brightest star in the constellation of Eridanus. There are many chairs in our world, but some shine brighter than others. —*Page 103*

The architects Federico Correa and Alfons Milà (1924–2009) were heirs of the Modern Movement and teachers of an important generation of Spanish designers, including the two-man team formed by Oscar Tusquets and Lluís Clotet. They designed the Reno chair in 1961 for a Barcelona restaurant by the same name. It was produced by the Gres firm until it closed in 1998. Their typological inspiration was the oval-backed Louis XV or Isabelline chair, which also inspired Starck years later when he designed the Louis Ghost chair for Kartell in 2002. —*Page 101*

Philippe Starck has proved that he has a rare talent for reworking and updating designs from the past that have become archetypes. With modern manufacturing technology, the collaboration of Eugeni Quitllet, and a healthy dose of irony, in 2009 he presented the Masters chair, also manufactured by Kartell, as a tribute to three historic chairs: the Series 7 by Arne Jacobson, the Tulip by Eero Saarinen, and the Eiffel by Charles and Ray Eames. The French designer introduced it with these words: "We weren't born just today. There have been masters before us. Putting them all together, they create a new product, a new project, like a reflection of our new society."

The Throne is Power

By Santi Barjau

The royal throne is undoubtedly the king of chairs. Even more than a crown or scepter, it symbolizes power: take the throne, keep the throne, lose the throne. We also use it in a figurative sense: who might dethrone the king of rock or the queen of pop? Religions have been made in the image of monarchies. Gods rule the world from their thrones. In the medieval art of Byzantine mosaics and Romanesque frescoes, and even in a famous panel painting by Van Eyck, we find an elliptical representation of divinity: an empty throne filled with rich cushions supporting the holy book. One such image is depicted in the Romanesque paintings of the little church of Sant Quirce de Pedret, in the Pyrenees. This image is known as *heitomasia* or "preparation," awaiting the second coming of Jesus, and is based on the ninth Psalm, which refers to a throne prepared for the implacable judge who will preside over the Last Judgment. An empty throne is sufficient to represent the Almighty.

A Mysterious Journey

By Mónica Piera

How did a chair from India make its way to the cloistered convent of Pedralbes in the sixteenth century? The famous Queen's Chair found in Barcelona remains an unsolved mystery.

This exceptional seat is made of cedar, lacquer, and rattan, all unfamiliar materials to a Europe that was just beginning to explore other continents. Moreover, although low chairs were often found on the daises of elegant Spanish ladies, the proportions of this specimen were foreign to our traditions.

To understand what this chair is doing in Pedralbes, we must bear in mind that the convent had accepted women of noble and even royal birth since its founding. The chair could have been part of the dowry brought by one of its more distinguished novices, perhaps someone related to the court of Philip II, who admired and collected exotic objects; but the fact that it is called the "Queen's Chair" suggests it may have been presented to the nunnery as a gift from a queen. The most plausible hypothesis is that it was given to Abbess Magdalena de Montcada by Margaret of Austria when she visited the convent with Philip III in 1599.

It is hard to imagine any abbess using it, as the unusually wide seat would have forced her to sit crossed-legged, in what Spaniards called the Moorish style. The Queen's Chair was probably valued and treated as a work of art, a privilege few seats can claim. We don't know which room it was kept in, but it must have been greatly admired for, in the seventeenth century, the convent's carpenter tried to imitate it and built a number of low sewing chairs—which would be used, unlike the original—inspired by the wonderful eastern piece. Although the form of the Catalan replicas does recall that of the model, the materials—painted black poplar and reeds—clearly identify them as local products.

The origin of the Queen's Chair proved quite difficult to trace, because no one suspected that a chair could have traveled such a long distance to end up in a cloistered nunnery. Now we know that this form corresponds to a type of throne common in southern Asia. The thick black lacquerwork with gilding is exquisite, made by artisans in the Bay of Bengal who catered exclusively to sultans and princes. Somehow, this chair left their hands and took a mysterious journey that ended on the Mother Abbess's doorstep.

The Power of a Chair

By María José Balcells

Has there ever been a more unusual throne than the one Mies van der Rohe designed for King Alfonso XIII and Queen Victoria Eugenie in 1929? The German Pavilion at the Barcelona World's Fair was expecting a royal visit, and the German architect and last director of the Bauhaus created his famous Barcelona chair to honor these two distinguished guests.

In 1929 Germany was already a world power, a modern country that prized innovation, and the pavilion Mies designed with Lilly Reich to represent his homeland was an accurate reflection of that modern zeal. It was an unconventional space, simple yet forceful, with gleaming walls of glass, onyx, and marble. The pavilion fairly exuded power, and the architect designed furniture deliberately calculated to reinforce that impression.

The chair he created for the pavilion had to be both ceremonial and restful. To fulfill the first requirement, Mies recalled the form of the curule chair used by Roman magistrates and drew an X-shaped frame. For the second, the architect gave it the shape and height of a lounge chair.

As with the pavilion, Mies applied the principles of the Bauhaus and his "less is more" maxim to the chair, simplifying it by reducing the structural elements to a minimum and echoing the gleam of the walls in the smooth, unbroken lines of its shiny steel legs. The cushions, made of horsehair and upholstered in leather, rested on leather or rubber webbing attached to the frame. The 1929 chairs were produced in white and in black, with buttons forming a diamond pattern on the cushions.

Despite its simple appearance, the Barcelona chair is heavy and solid, and although it was inspired by models for easy lounging, it is neither comfortable nor ergonomic. It was designed for a specific setting and, like the pavilion, really had only one purpose: empowerment. This may explain why Mies himself helped establish the legend of the throne, but the fact is that this chair was never intended or used as such.

After seven months at the fair, the chairs returned to Germany, and a few more were made in the 1930s. But it wasn't until 1947, when Mies van der Rohe was already settled in the United States, that the mighty Knoll International began to mass-produce them in earnest. The Barcelona chair been on the market ever since, and it's still a ceremonial status symbol. We find it in the offices of major corporations and banks, seats of power meant to impress, not to live in.

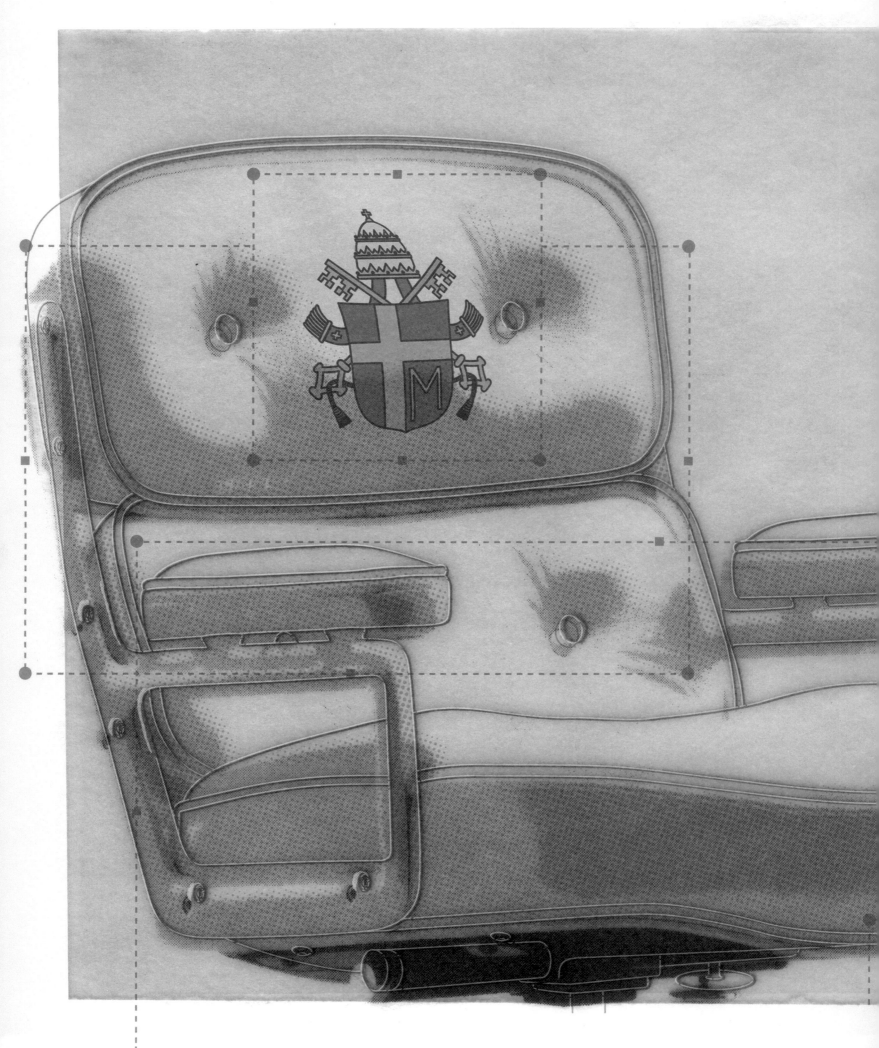

The Pope's Chair

By Ana Domínguez

It was on a business trip to the Herman Miller factory in an unfamiliar city: Grand Rapids, Michigan. We were accompanied by the designer Yves Behar, who was working with the American manufacturer on a new office chair. They gave us a tour of the facilities and we ended up in a basement where all sorts of products were stored: prototypes, special pieces, etc. While rummaging around, Yves and I lifted a plastic sheet and saw a white leather chair with a strange crest on the back. It was a model designed by Charles and Ray Eames called the Executive chair or Time-Life chair (because it was created for the Time-Life Building in 1960), with a back made of three pieces, instead of the usual two, and casters on the legs.

Curiosity got the better of us, and our investigation turned up an interesting fact: the chair had been a special commission made for Pope John Paul II in 1990. They customized it for him in soft white leather and gave it a higher back, marked with the distinctive red and blue papal crest. Apparently, the folks at Herman Miller were later informed that the pope had been delighted with his new office chair. Did Benedict keep it, or has it been passed on to Francis?

Seats of Power

The curule chair was reserved for prominent public authorities in ancient Rome. Viewed from the front, it has the same profile as the Barcelona chair that Ludwig Mies van der Rohe designed two millennia later for the same purpose. The name reflects the fact that it was part of the furniture made for the German Pavilion at the 1929 World's Fair in Barcelona. In 1930, Josef Müller began to manufacture and sell it in Berlin. Later the Bamburg Company took over production, and from 1932 to 1934 it was listed in the Thonet catalogue. It changed hands several times until Knoll purchased the rights and began producing it in 1947.

Mies van der Rohe (1886–1969) coined the famous phrase "Less is more," which summed up his modern vision of architecture. He also gave us other memorable quotes, such as "God is in the details" or "A chair is a very difficult object. A skyscraper is almost easier. That is why Chippendale is famous." —*Page 113*

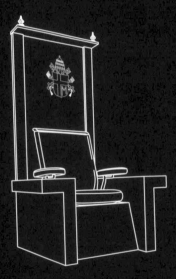

The Executive Work chair or Time-Life chair, as it was originally called, was designed for Herman Miller by Charles and Ray Eames in 1960.

The proof of a design's importance lies in the people who use it and the spaces it occupies. Chairs from the Eames Aluminum Group series can be found everywhere from offices to TV studios, but political and financial decision-making centers are their natural habitat.

Special edition for John Paul II made in 1990. —*Page 115*

John Paul II visited no less than 129 different countries during his papacy, which explains why he was nicknamed "the traveling pope." In 1994, on the occasion of his visit to the Croatian city of Zagreb, a modern papal throne was designed for him: the wooden frame stood 6 feet high and had a built-in white leather office seat. Oddly enough, it had the same upholstered armrests as the Executive chair; perhaps the head of the Catholic Church had grown used to them and made a special request. The piece was included in the *Seats of Power* exhibition curated by Heng Zhi and held at the Vitra Design Museum in 2018.

When Pope Benedict xvi visited the Spanish city of Valencia in 2006 to close the World Meeting of Families, an altar was erected in the City of Arts and Sciences to celebrate mass.

The stage was designed by architect Juan Pablo Mas, and Andreu World was commissioned to design and build a new papal throne, a hand-crafted piece of solid beech wood with walnut details and white upholstery. The technical drawings show the back surmounted by a semicircular arch where the Vatican crest would go. After the pontiff's visit, this one-of-a-kind creation became the property of the Valencian church.

Andreu World was also asked to supply other chairs for the monarchs, government officials, and ecclesiastical authorities who would sit on stage near the altar. It rose to the occasion with a special edition of the Cloé chair designed by Lievore Altherr Molina.

Sitting Down to Take a Stand

By Guillem Celada

In the 1950s, the buses that provided public transportation in the town of Montgomery, Alabama—and probably almost every other city across the United States—had seats made of chrome-plated iron tubes. The frame of those aligned benches, designed to hold two people, supported seated passengers, but they also gave those who had to stand or move around inside the vehicle something to hold on to. This type of construction, with curved iron tubing screwed in place, recalls the exemplary chair designs of the modern Bauhausians and their contemporaries.

The seat that covered the iron frame had shock-absorbing springs to make the ride less bumpy. These seats and their backs were upholstered in dark, hard-wearing, pleather-like plastic.

Like so many other chairs in history, these plain, functional city bus seats had become a status symbol—in this case, because they were off-limits to black passengers.

Paradoxically, the absurdity of this ban was suddenly exposed by someone who used the seat as it was intended to be used. Not by standing on it like a soapbox to denounce injustice, not by tearing it loose and tossing it out of the vehicle in protest, but simply by sitting down and refusing to relinquish it to a white passenger. On December 1, 1955, Mrs. Rosa Parks remained seated and ushered in a new era in the African American struggle for civil rights.

Her act of defiance got her kicked off the bus in mid-route and tried for violating the city's segregation laws, which sparked a 382-day boycott of Montgomery buses, but it was worth it: the courageous and serene Mrs. Parks had proved that you can take a stand by sitting down.

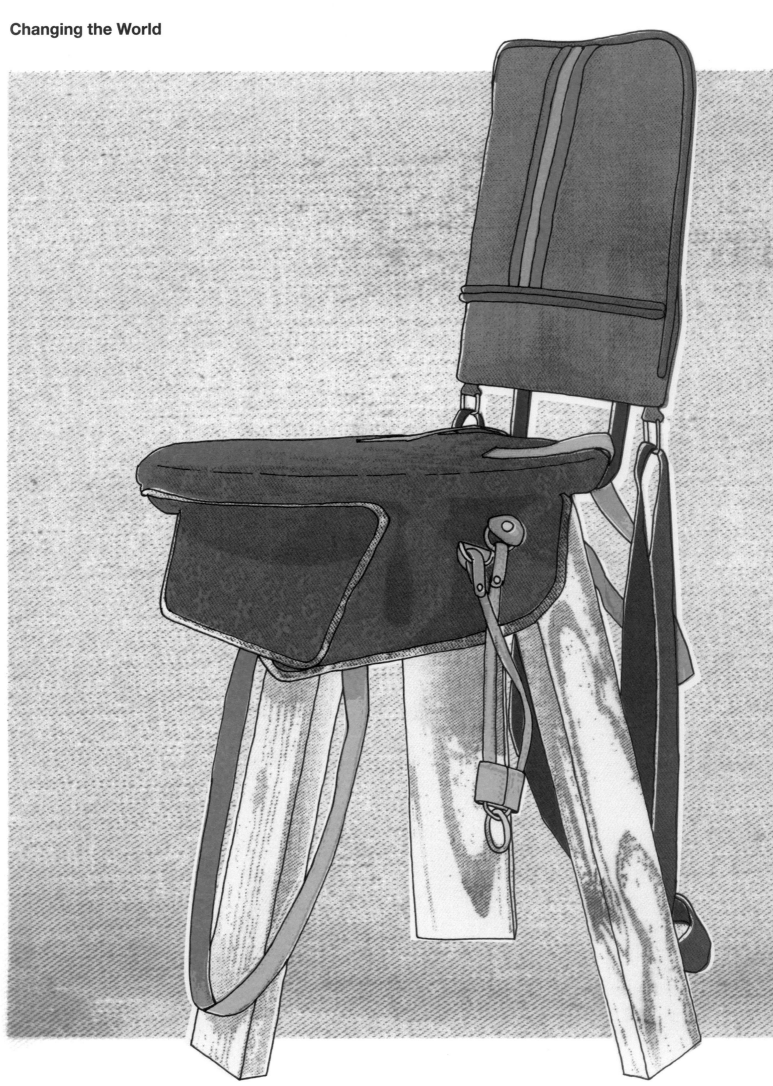

Curro Claret Says His "Piece"

By Ramón Úbeda

There's a certain class of designers who work to build a better society and have managed to trade selfishness for altruism. I know one. He's called Curro, and with a name like that—*curro* is informal for "I work" in Spanish—I'd hazard a guess that he was predestined to do what he does. He's spent more than twenty years proving that design can also be a very useful tool for helping others, coming up with simple ideas that, oddly enough, never occurred to any of his professional colleagues. Those ideas serve the common good, and especially the most disadvantaged, like the homeless people who live or have lived on the street, excluded from society and seemingly invisible to everyone except him.

I don't know of anyone else who dared to go before a church authority and propose replacing the pews with others of his own design that also serve to worship and pray, but which at night can become a much-needed bed for those who have nowhere to sleep. That project was called "For the Love of God." Irony is often necessary to stir the consciences of those who could do more for the denizens of this underworld, but Curro Claret feels right at home among them and has never needed a nudge. The list of initiatives and projects he's launched is long, and one of them is particularly fitting for this book because no one has ever designed a seat like his.

He calls it "The Piece" and it doesn't look like much: just a plain metal sheet, laser-cut, perforated, and bent. But if you let someone use its holes to screw on a plank, a board, or some other piece of scrap wood, then it becomes a chair, a stool, or a bench. And that's exactly what the underprivileged people served by Arrels Fundació do in the foundation's workshop. The money they make selling this furniture helps mitigate their situation, but the profits are not just financial: participating in a creative activity makes them feel like productive members of society again, bringing them one step closer to reintegration.

They design the furniture based on the piece that Curro provides, whose aim is to reunite and retrieve what others have discarded. It also gives visibility to a persistent yet often overlooked problem. Since beginning this project, Curro has held several furniture shows with "The Piece," including one at Sala Vinçon in 2014 that consisted entirely of chairs. Curro prepared an auxiliary piece so that a backrest could be added to the chairs and invited different people—from a sex worker to scrap metal collectors—to design their own seats using whatever resources and materials were at hand. My favorites are the one with iron burn marks created by a woman in domestic service and the one made from knock-off designer bags by an unlicensed street vendor.

Sedia 1

By Albert Fuster

A strange object assaults the expert eye. Supposedly, it's a kit for assembling a simple chair from wood laths and boards. We're given basic multiview illustrations—plan, elevation, profile—and an isometric projection. The measurements of each piece are provided in a handwritten table, like carpenter's notes. Only the isometric view shows where the nails go, the only joints in a design that avoids dovetails and glues.

The kit is part of the *Proposta per un'autoprogettazione* that Enzo Mari introduced in 1973 and presented at Galleria Milano the following year. It seems to sum up Mari's life experiences—dramatic poverty in childhood, self-educated outside the channels of formal schooling, more creator and builder than designer—and his reaction to a design industry dominated by images and consumerism. After the second postwar period and the closure of the Ulm school, western European design seemed incapable of operating outside the confines of the dominant capitalist system.

But Mari fought back with an object that makes a statement like few pieces have done in the history of design.

Design may be the fundamental tool of capitalist consumerism.

The designer's identity may only be a means of finding the formal codes that appeal to mass consumers.

The global market may be an abstract world where the flow and exchange of commodities is boundless, limited only by their economic value.

Mari counters these suspicions by offering us his *Autoprogettazione*: a design that goes beyond all forms, all aesthetic experiences, all sociocultural constraints. He invites us to live in the world as a concrete experience.

Fishing Lessons

By Ramón Úbeda

If you happen to be traveling in southern Senegal and make your way to the town of Thionck Essyl, you may come across a sign that reads CEM Kamanar. This secondary school deserves to be featured in a guide to good deeds, for its architecture and for what it has made possible. The modular classrooms were designed in Barcelona using a system based on the inverted catenary arch and built by locals from compressed earth blocks made on site. The architects and a team of volunteers, coordinated by the Foundawtion and led by David García and Luis Morón, patiently showed them how to do it.

It took nearly five years to complete the project. They could have finished sooner if they'd shipped in prefabricated huts, but it wouldn't have been the same. That would have been charity, and, as the old Chinese proverb says, you're not helping much if you give a poor man a fish.

The point is to share knowledge that facilitates independent development, and it has to be a two-way street. This project was a journey where two cultures met halfway and worked together to raise a building; visitors and locals sank their feet into the same mud and applied their hands to the same tasks. And what's good for the container also applies to the contents, because a school requires more than just a roof: it needs furniture to accommodate the students.

This school has nearly five hundred pupils, and they all need a place to sit. Marc Morro designed all the furniture for this place, applying the same logic that inspired the architect to use a Catalan vault: not to export it to Africa, but because it's a form that's easy to build using local materials and methods, sustainable, and efficient in that climate. Marc wanted to know exactly what kind of woods and resources were available there, and he made it very easy for Lamine, the local carpenter, by devising a system for making furniture so simple that he doesn't even need a measuring tape. In other words, he taught him how to fish without having to use a rod. The most remarkable piece is the chair, which also played a part in raising funds to finance this project.

From Aversion to Fascination

By Carmen Sevilla

After an operation, I needed a wheelchair to get around. In addition to the difficulties of moving about in a world that definitely doesn't make life easy for people with mobility issues, I've discovered how inhospitable most wheelchairs are. I must admit that the very sight of one makes me uncomfortable, and I immediately sense my body tensing up. Why does this happen, if it's an object designed to improve my quality of life, to enable me to go outside, enjoy a stroll, an afternoon at the movies, or a dinner with friends?

I've tried three different chair models. I've never quite worked out what the percentages used to rate wheelchair ergonomics mean: the seats are uncomfortable and the backs are pure torture; you can't adjust the footrests to suit the nature of your ailment or overcome the obstacle of curbs; shock absorbency is nonexistent; sitting in them leaves me aching all over; and I could go on and on.

But analyzing their functionality still doesn't tell me why the mere sight of a wheelchair upsets me, even though I need it. This is where the intangible factors of design come into play: aesthetics and symbolic and emotional values. The sight of a wheelchair makes us think of illness, old age, decrepitude, health problems, difficulties, suffering, dependence, etc. How can the forms of an object designed to help convey the exact opposite of its intended purpose?

After two years working in partnership with the digital software company 3D Materialise, Benjamin Hubert and his London agency, Layer, designed the GO chair. My first reaction upon seeing it was fascination—fascination with its forms, lines, finishes, textures. It's a wheelchair that has aesthetic appeal, a design that conveys movement, agility, lightness, elegance, trendiness, technology. I realized that I wasn't looking at a medical device but a private vehicle that would improve my quality of life. The company spent six months working with wheelchair users and medical specialists, and from this they learned that, in addition to considering the functional aspects, they needed to remove the stigma associated with wheelchairs.

As 15-year-old Lizzy said, "You want a chair that's practical during the day but also looks cool when you head out to the club at night with your friends."

Sitting Tight

By Albert Fuster

Only in Western culture do we automatically associate sitting with chairs. There's whole other world out there with infinite possible forms, postures and objects that don't assume a seat has to be a horizontal surface two hand spans above the ground. This Western notion is not just a trivial formalization or the result of an artisanal or industrial process; it's also a reflection of historical social relations, as Sigfried Giedion and Norbert Elias have proved in various essays. Kings, nobles, politicians, judges, bosses, professors, and dinner guests have used the chair as a visible affirmation of rank, separation, and power.

Architect Alejandro Aravena created a "sitting device" for Vitra. Apparently inspired by something invented by South American Indians, the device is a textile strap that wraps around the back and knees to stabilize the body and relieve tension, allowing users to sit comfortably on the floor while leaving their hands free for other things. It's ideal for festivals, airports, public spaces, parks and suburban beaches, the typical spaces of a nomadic contemporary world where class distinctions are increasingly blurred and questioned.

In the midst of a global economic crisis, Aravena came up with this solution for a generation that's no longer willing to sit tight and wait for things to change, a generation that rejects the idea of spaces and objects as status symbols. The Chairless announces that the disappearance of the chair has triggered a sequence of events which will transform the social relations we've built up around it, and no one knows how or where it will end...

Inflatable Utopia

By Isabel Campi

Anyone who has designed or produced a chair knows how hard it is to come up with a structure that looks light as air yet is strong enough to support a corpulent person's weight. You have to camouflage how the powerful forces of tension and torsion act on the structure. For millennia, chairs had four legs. Using steel tubes, Modern Movement designers made do with two, and in the mid-1950s Eero Saarinen managed to rest his Tulip chair on a single leg, making it look like a pedestal. The next challenge was to design a legless chair—in other words, a chair floating on air.

The dream came true in the 1960s, when it was discovered that high frequency welded PVC film could be used to make efficient inflatable structures. The concept wasn't new: inflatable structures like hot-air balloons, zeppelins, and lifeboats had been tried and tested for years. But with new technology, inexpensive mass production became possible. Pop designers and architects were searching for alternatives to concrete and steel construction systems that would express their rejection of modern academicism, and the perfected pneumatic devices let their imaginations run wild. Inflatables were the ideal vehicle for conveying the concepts of the ephemeral and transitory, and in many ways they were one of Pop's most original statements. Pneumatic buildings and objects accurately reflected the younger generation's desire to cast off conventional notions of solidity and permanence.

During the heyday of Pop, inflatable structures were "in the air," so the Musée d'Art Moderne in Paris invited the Utopie collective to mount an exhibition titled *Structures gonflables* in 1968—coincidentally, the same year as the student revolution. Utopie was a group of young French architects led by Henri Lefebvre, a city planner with Marxist leanings, who challenged the mediocrity of modern urbanism, architecture, and design by proposing inflatable pavilions and cities that could be set up and taken down in a matter of hours, at any location, and without prior notice. Three members of the group—Jean Aubert, Jean-Paul Jungmann, and Antoine Stinco—founded a company called A.J.S. Aérolande to produce and sell their "airy" furniture. Unlike the British group Archigram, which also designed inflatable cities but never ventured beyond their graphic utopia, Aérolande had a social vision and wanted to make their designs available to people in the real world.

One of their most successful and widely imitated furniture designs was the Tore chair, first issued in 1968. Structurally, it consisted of two air "sausages" wrapped around an ottoman also filled with air. The hollow space inside was clearly visible thanks to the use of transparent plastic which, combined with the absence of color and the simple mechanics of inflation, produced a plump, puffy armchair: highly entertaining, quite uncomfortable, and as evanescent as its creators' ideals.

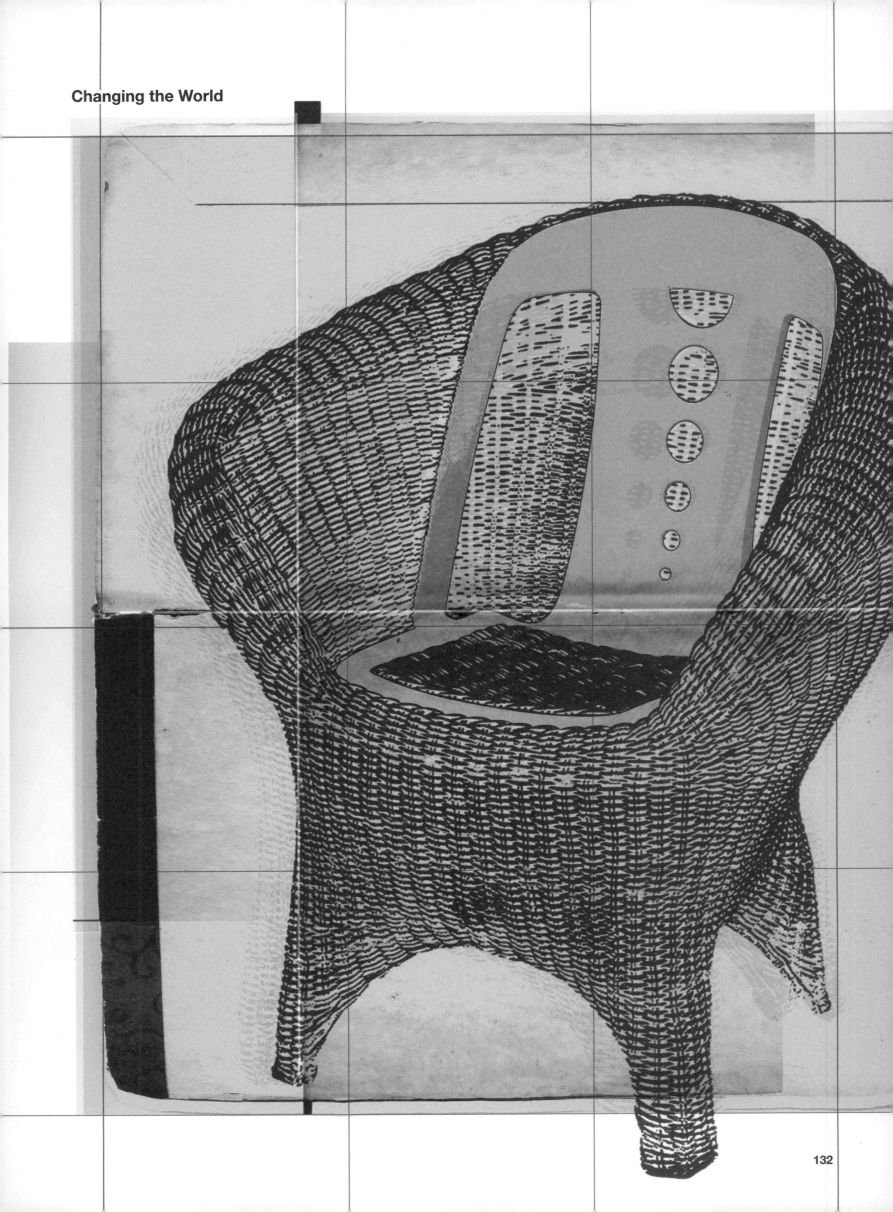

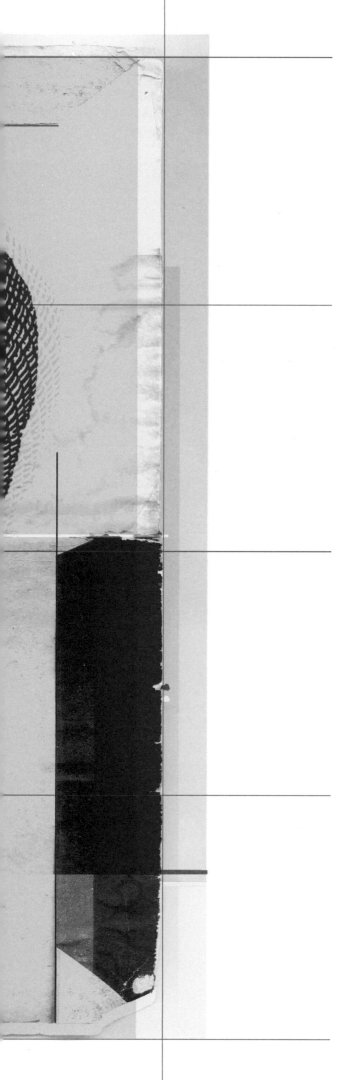

Ecological Counterattack

By Ana Domínguez

I ran into Fernando and Humberto Campana during a summer workshop at Boisbuchet. We had time for long conversations over meals shared at communal tables, the highlight of the country life everyone leads in that place. One afternoon we got to talking about their TransPlastic collection, undoubtedly the one that best expresses the Brazilian brothers' way of thinking. Manual craftsmanship as opposed to industrial production, how to take humble local materials—in this case a fiber called *apuí*—and ennoble them by using design to give them an unexpected beauty. A lot has been said about this project, where the designers took those ghastly, poorly made plastic chairs that are unfortunately invading the planet, and transformed them by weaving them into new, handcrafted structures whose organic forms seem to grow naturally around a foreign object.

"To be honest," they told me, "the idea came from our mother. She had the habit of sitting outside in the street to chat with her friends. As we were getting famous and becoming known around the world, we told her she couldn't keep sitting on that horrible plastic chair." They wanted to design a new one for her, but she refused, saying she was content with her chair and telling them to stop pestering her. So, they decided to take that chair and work it into a manual process in which the fibers appear to overpower the plastic. The result is a hybrid form that resembles a war cry, announcing an ecological counterattack on a world overrun by plastic. And mama was happy because she got to keep her chair.

The Non Conformist Chair

By Carmen Sevilla

I can't decide if I want a comfortable chair with armrests, or one without them so I can make a quick escape from an awkward meeting. I've been in that situation of wanting to slip away discreetly but knowing that, if I moved my chair, everyone's eyes would inevitably turn to me. Eileen Gray's Non Conformist Chair offers the solution to my dilemma and embodies the mocking, humane, creative spirit of its author.

Designed in 1925, it's surprisingly original and daring. Made of tubular steel, like the pieces designed by her contemporaries Stam and Breuer, this chair seems to challenge the Modern Movement's concept of geometry and rationality. Its emphatic asymmetry and unapologetic bulkiness defied the rationalist masters. The most modern of modernists, its creator went beyond functionalist premises and tried to meet the user's most intimate needs, humanizing her design with ergonomics and irony.

"I'm serious, professional, responsible, and reliable, but I'm also bold, restless, fast, and changeable. I'm a woman of the fast-paced twentieth century; we've survived the Great War; I have to be free, daring, fun, and attuned to these modern times." I can imagine Eileen Gray saying these words and adapting the Non Conformist Chair's forms to the contradictory desires of its user. The chair embodies those two sides of the same coin: it's functional and comfortable, but also fun, personal, and unique. Her work in the 1920s foreshadowed the postmodern challenges of the 1980s and the emotional design of the turn of the millennium. Her freedom, curiosity, professionalism, and audacity were both highly admired and bitterly envied by the great figures of her day.

I can imagine myself escaping from the tedious meeting, slipping silently out the armless side, or letting my body slump on the padded armrest when I succumb to tedium, exhaustion, or apathy.

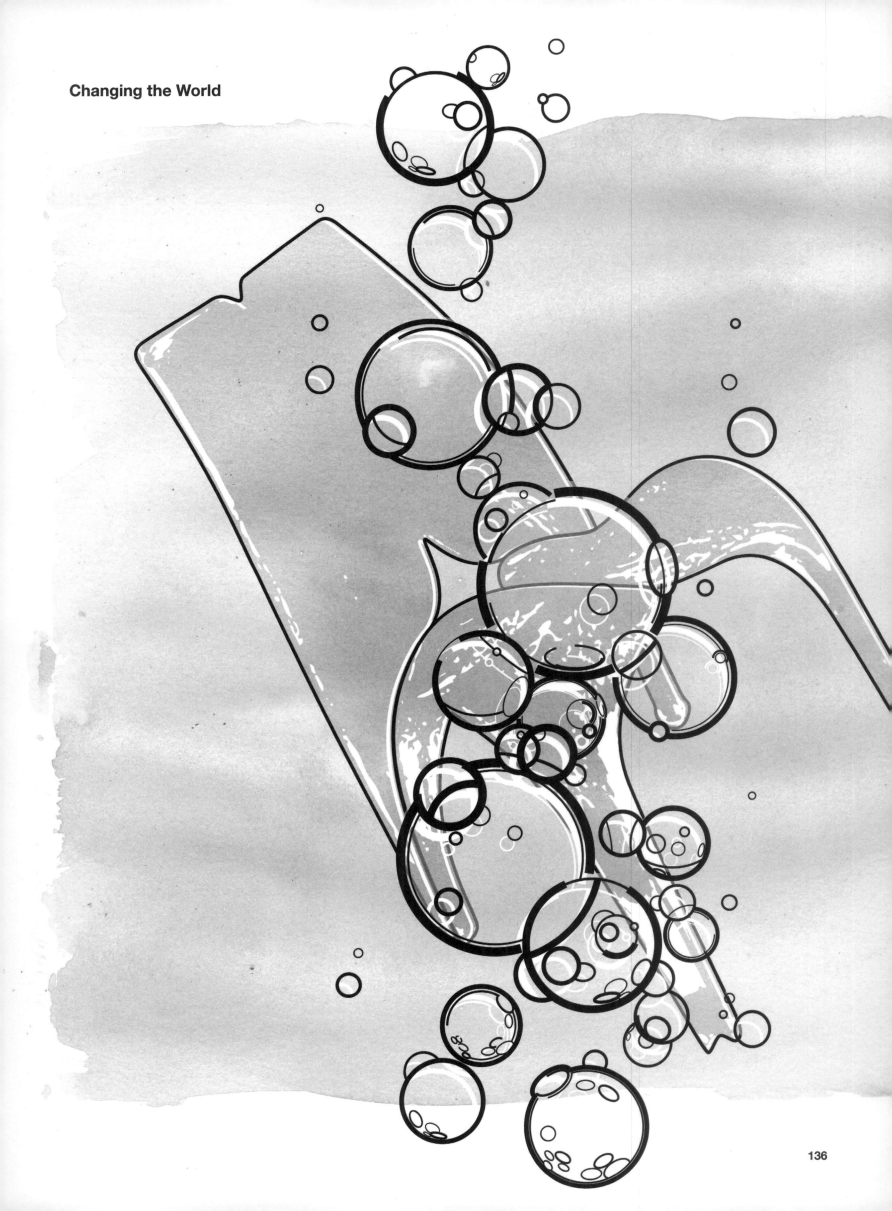

The Liquid Chair

By Rosalía Torrent

Liquid modernity, liquid life, liquid love... The liquid reality described by Polish essayist Zygmunt Bauman has finally found a chair to sit in: a liquid one, of course. It's the Liquid Glacial by Zaha Hadid. Bauman described the new social scenario as one that invites movement and, like water, embraces the concepts of fluidity, adaptation, and change. Not so long ago, the world was predictable and resistant to change, but now it's starting to "liquefy," becoming malleable. That world of "solids" has given way to another of "liquids," and, as Bauman notes, liquids are not easily stopped.

Hadid's architecture undoubtedly reflects the malleable sentiment of the new modernity. As if wanting to venture into the new liquid spirit, she left a memento in Spain: her Bridge Pavilion for Expo 2008 Zaragoza. During the fair, that pavilion hosted an exhibition called *Water, a Unique Resource*, which warned of the gradual depletion of the earth's water reserves. It seemed premonitory.

The Liquid Glacial chair really should have been made of water, but for now it's impossible—as impossible as realizing the Bauhausian dream of sitting on columns of air. Inventors haven't yet figured out how to achieve those two visions. But Hadid didn't give up. It wasn't in her nature. And after all, she had acrylic or poly(methyl-methacrylate), a rigid and exceptionally transparent thermoplastic. She turned acrylic into water—or, more accurately, frozen water. Glacial liquid.

It wasn't the first time the architect had made furniture from this material and with these particular characteristics. She made design, or perhaps art—or, more likely, a hybrid of both. And the results are stunning. It's almost impossible to approach them in a conventional setting. They were born to be in an art gallery. David Gill's proverbial instincts told him to take them to his gallery near the Christie's auction house in London. This Zaragoza native who immigrated to London, a dandy in the cradle of dandyism, couldn't help falling in love with the Anglo-Iraqi's work. After Hadid's untimely passing, Gill has tirelessly honored her memory by making her designs visible. This chair will undoubtedly have a long life, as all works overflowing with creativity do. The diamond of the organic glitters in the ersatz ice of these forms.

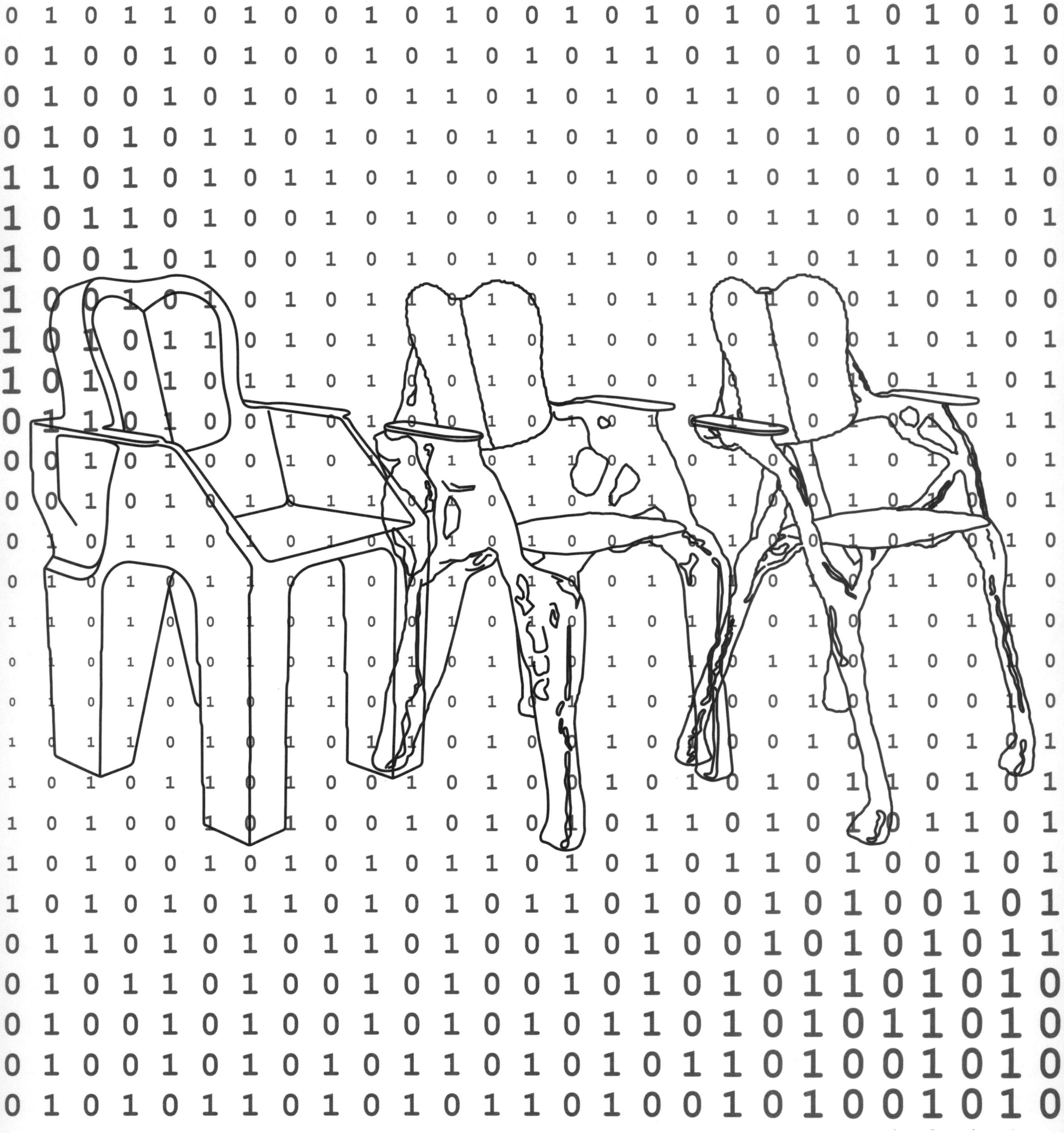

Artificial Intelligence

By Carmen Sevilla

Can you imagine an object where your body could sit and rest without being conditioned by your knowledge and experience of chairs, or without the very concept of the chair imposing limits and boundaries? This is the kind of challenge designers often put to themselves to stimulate their creativity, and it's certainly not easy.

Who could come up with such an object? Where can we find an intelligence impervious to our cultural archetypes? An extraterrestrial intelligence, perhaps? But, although these ideas verge on science fiction, we don't have to cross over into pure fantasy.

Philippe Starck has dared to imagine a different way of designing. He prides himself on not owning a computer, because he believes his creativity would be limited to the environment and processes that other human beings have imagined he might need. However, he was interested in working with a new collaborator: artificial intelligence. A.I. is not a closed environment that simply obeys and executes human commands; it responds to queries by coming up with its own proposals. The A.I. chair is the result of that collaboration.

Instead of drawing the object, the designer simply wrote a brief and specified the injection molding production requirements of the manufacturer, Kartell. The solutions were supplied by artificial intelligence using generative design algorithms. Basically, it replied to the simple question, "How can you support our body with the least amount of material and energy possible?" without influence, without memory, using only its own mathematical intelligence. And it simulated and tested various possibilities in record time until finding the optimal solution.

This fires my imagination. What things might this new collaborator create that human intelligence can't even imagine? What happens when that intelligence acquires emotional as well as rational abilities, when it can feel, when it has a personality and preferences?

Starck once said that his job is useless, and today that strikes me as rather prophetic... Is he playing with fire by opening the door to a designer that could outstrip human creativity and natural intelligence? If that happens, what will be the designer's role? Are we heading toward a utopian or dystopian future of design?

Changing the World

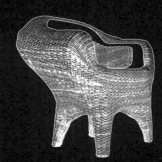

Eileen Gray (1878–1976) survived two world wars and lived to be nearly one hundred. She was born in Ireland, opened her first furniture store in London in 1915 with Japanese lacquer master Seizo Sugawara, and lived in Paris for most of her life. An architect and elegant designer, Gray was one of the first women to be recognized and admired in her profession. Of all the art movements and styles she saw emerge, she was especially influenced by De Stijil and the Bauhaus, with their nonconformist spirit and desire to reinvent architecture and modern furniture design. —*Page 135*

The Campana brothers presented their TransPlastic series at the Albion Gallery, London, in 2007. The combination of natural and artificial elements yielded furniture that makes a powerful statement. Traditional wicker outdoor furniture has gradually been replaced by cheap plastic chairs. Their project draws attention to this fact, making it clear that artisanal work offers lovelier results and sending a message about the importance of sustainability. The fiber used, *apuí*, is a typical Brazilian plant that suffocates and kills the trees from which it grows. Its extraction helps preserve and control the biodiversity of the forests. —*Page 133*

Alejandro Aravena is a Chilean architect who won the Pritzker Prize in 2016 for his public housing work and his extensive and remarkable architectural portfolio. However, he has never presented a furniture design. The Chairless device he created for Vitra in 2010, based on the sitting straps used by the Ayoreo tribe in Paraguay, is more like a manifesto than a piece of furniture. —*Page 129*

Enzo Mari is one of the great names that wrote the history of twentieth-century design. He won the Compasso d'Oro Award four times, two of which were for his Delfina (1979) and Tonietta chairs (1987). In 1974 he published and freely distributed the *Autoprogettazione* manual, which included several models of tables, chairs, beds, and shelves, basic household furniture pieces that only needed wood, nails, and a hammer to assemble. Mari's message has grown more powerful over the years, and the Sedia 1 has become a banner of social, sustainable design. In 2010, Artek began selling the kit for those too lazy to find their own materials. —*Page 123*

Curro Claret studied Industrial Design at the Elisava School, Barcelona, and Central Saint Martins, London. In 2010, he participated in a competition organized by the Spanish Ministries of Culture and Health, called "Design against Poverty." He came up with "The Piece," a simple metal structure for assembling and building furniture with recycled materials. He won a prize and used the money to develop a line of stools, tables, and lamps that illustrated its possibilities, in collaboration with the Arrels Fundació workshop. He then made his idea available to anyone who requested it, provided the furniture was made by more or less underprivileged social groups as a means of helping them in their difficult situation. —*Page 121*

Marc Morro was born in Mallorca and moved to Barcelona, where he and his partner Oriol Villar run the AOO furniture company. The first two designs they produced were the Manolito stool and the Pepitu deckchair, in the simple Mediterranean style they like their chairs to have. In summer 2018, DadàBarcelona organized a children's workshop about the chair Marc had designed for a school in Senegal. In a few hours, the kids constructed and painted thirty-six chairs, with the help of various artists, which they later sold to help raise funds. —*Page 125*

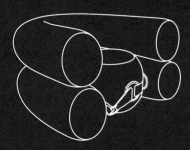

The Tore armchair was produced in 1968 by A.J.S. Aérolande. The Centre Pompidou in Paris has a collection of more than two hundred inflatable furniture pieces made between 1960 and 1975. —*Page 131*

Zaha Hadid (1950–2016) was born in Baghdad, spent most of her life in London, and set out to revolutionize the world of architecture. It took time and patience to make her ideas a reality. Rolf Fehlbaum sponsored her first building project in 1993, the fire station on the Vitra Campus, the capital of chair culture. It was the beginning of her unstoppable rise to stardom. In 2004, she became the first woman to receive the Pritzker Prize. Like her buildings, her furniture designs evolved toward increasingly fluid forms. The Liquid Glacial collection, made in 2015 for David Gill's gallery, was one of her last projects. —*Page 137*

French designer Philippe Starck began his career in the 1980s, and the number of seats he's designed since then could fill a separate *Chairpedia*. He's always been ahead of the pack in his use of technology and his message of sustainability and democratic design, though he has also created his share of exclusive and futuristic projects. Starck has worked for NASA, Axiom Space, Virgin Galactic, and Steve Jobs, for whom he designed a "galactic" yacht. In 2018 he presented A.I. as "the first chair designed outside of the human brain." Autodesk software was used to "materialize" it. —*Page 139*

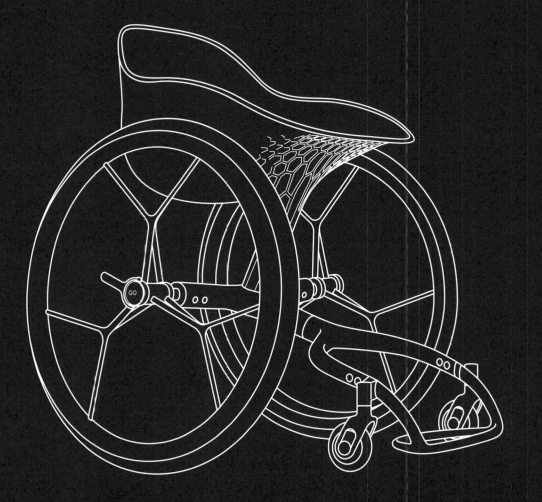

The seat and foot-bay of the GO wheelchair, designed by Benjamin Hubert in 2016, are printed in 3D after mapping each user's biometric information to ensure an ergonomic and comfortable product. Each chair is adapted to the person's weight, body shape, and disability. The seat is printed in two plastics for better shock absorption and calculates the center of gravity based on the user's weight. It can be manufactured and delivered in less than two weeks. The mobility mechanism was also considered, designing special gloves that lock into the push rims for extra grip. —*Page 127*

Mrs. Bates's Rocking Chair

By Oriol Pibernat

A rocker is just a rocker, unless it ends up in an Alfred Hitchcock movie. Mrs. Bates's rocking chair (*Psycho*, 1960) was lucky enough to be cast alongside the film's "living" stars—and, of course, Norman Bates's deceased mother. Hitchcockian suspense and terror is often based on moral ambiguity and an innate amphibology of persons and things; guileless, squeaky-clean people and objects suddenly become guilty and sinister (and vice versa).

The sight of an affable old lady on her front porch, crocheting and rocking gently in a chair, is one thing. The revelation of a psychopath's basement shrine where he keeps his mother's corpse propped in a rocking chair is quite another. As the king of visual synecdoche, Hitchcock managed to condense the ghosts that haunted the human mind in a single image of a Victorian mansion. This was the preferred iconography on the posters that advertised the film in 1960. That motel brought the horrors of the House of Usher into the twentieth century and became the inspiration for every self-respecting haunted house at an amusement park. However, for the publicity photos, the director used another object and posed the actors as if they were being stalked by the shadow of a rocker. *

Here we see our vindicated rocking chair in its successful role as a set prop essential to the plot—though in fact this isn't even the model used in the film. The rocker has the same menacing appearance as the mansion, perhaps because of its prosaic shabbiness and misshapen proportions. In any event, it doesn't have the understated elegance of a Windsor or the distinction of a colonial rocking chair, or even the harmonious simplicity of a Shaker rocker. No, it doesn't seem to boast a pedigree, but the silhouette of its turned spindles and ornamental openwork looms as ominously as Nosferatu's shadow.

At the deepest level of our subconscious fears lurks the suspicion that objects may have a soul. Far from an alien belief, animism still dogs our footsteps. And, faced with the grim image of a hunchbacked chair... we begin to think it may catch up with us.

*Alfred Hitchcock used all kinds of distracting ploys to promote the film's premiere without giving away the plot, and one was a photo session with the stars of *Psycho*: Janet Leigh, Vera Miles, John Gavin, and the good old rocking chair (as the authorized stand-in for Anthony Perkins and Mrs. Bates).

The Chair and the Uncanny

By Rosalía Torrent

This is the story of a young philosophy student named Nataniel. One of his go-to authors was Freud, and one of his favorite themes, the uncanny. In his essay on this aesthetic category, the father of psychoanalysis mentions a story by Hoffman, "The Sand-Man," in which the main character is named Nathaniel, like our student. Maybe that's why he liked it. Either that, or because humans are irresistibly drawn to the uncanny as the epitome of an unsettling paradox, where the familiar becomes strange and the strange takes on the guise of familiarity.

That morning, Nataniel found himself in the Swiss city of Chur, having come there from Zurich, where he was finishing his studies. With a history that dates back millennia, Chur is considered the oldest town in the little Alpine country. It's also home to the Giger Bar, a place he was eager to visit. Created by Swiss artist Hans Ruedi Giger, this bar offers a unique experience. Ceilings, floors, and walls, accessories, furniture: everything is shaped by the imagination of this author, to whom we also owe the extraterrestrial presence in the film *Alien*. Ridley Scott, its director, was already acquainted with Giger and the Harkonnen chairs project, a visual manifesto of the uncanny and sinister side of life.

These chairs were initially designed to serve as a necessary prop for Baron Harkonnen, a character in Frank Herbert's science fiction novel *Dune* which Alejandro Jodorowsky planned to make into a movie. That film was never produced (although David Lynch eventually shot another version, this time without Giger). But the chairs had already been made, although the heinous villain would never sit on them.

But the bar's patrons did. And so did our young student, who saw Freudian theories in those pieces designed with the organic sinuousness of the living and constant references to death. He settled into the inky blackness of the main chair, Capo, with its arms and its crown of three skulls; the other seats in the series lack the former or the latter, but still maintain the grim illusion. A pelvis instead of skulls cradles the unborn.

Today few people could afford to buy one of the costly fiberglass or aluminum replicas of these chairs. But it doesn't matter. Nataniel nurses a drink as he thinks of the film that never was: of Salvador Dalí, who would have had to play the part of the galactic Padishah Emperor Shaddam; and of Gaudí, whose organic style inhabits these forms. In the end, he decided to set out for Gruyères, another Swiss town where a new Giger Bar opened in 2003. He's determined to soak up its essence.

The Royal Garden Chair

By Oriol Pibernat

The Royal Garden chair is little more than a stool with a back. But what a back! An ethereal support of tubular steel rods rising to a crown whose five points are each topped by a sphere (just like the Rolex logo). The motif is repeated on the light sconces, though these are more harmless; on the chairs, the design caused collateral damage. We hear the manager of the venue, which is opening that very night, berate the decorator: "Mind your job. The chairs leave marks. Do something about it immediately." And it's true: when the diners stand up, they've got that crown stamped on their dinner jackets and blazers.

The Royal Garden chair in Jacques Tati's *Playtime* (1967) is a gentle mockery: the chair, the restaurant, and the entire city of Tativille. It's all part of the vast set Tati constructed to give the everyday a slight twist, bring a half-smile to our lips, and make us see the ridiculous side of modern city life, the myths of consumerism, progress, and design—the legendary icons of the 1960s. The chair is just one of the many trinkets or gag props that populate this and other films by Tati. * Yet this chair is particularly ludicrous because it combines the aspirations of fashion and ancestry. It is the crest of the *nouveau riche*, a gaudy garnish, a rubber-stamp seal that has rather the same effect as a "kick me" sign stuck to someone's back on April Fools' Day. In the scenes shot at the Royal Garden, Tati revels in offering us a glimpse of how this great sham is built up and torn down. The middle-class delusions of grandeur even seem rather endearing, especially when plans go awry. This happens when the elaborate physical and social facade collapses, a disaster brought on by the confusion of the norm, the sudden evaporation of etiquette, and the dazed awkwardness Hulot's mere presence triggers.

In the same movie, other gags involve chairs. The farting sounds of the Tativille office chairs still strike me as a vaporous yet impertinent human revenge on the gods of architecture. Specifically, one of the dourest, Mies van der Rohe, and one of the most conceited, Le Corbusier.

* The set and props of this and other Tati films were designed by the director himself in collaboration with Jacques Lagrange.

Movie Designs

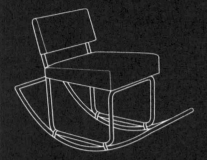

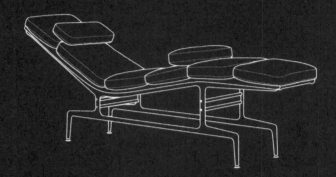

Jacques Tati is probably one of the few—if not the only—film directors who designed chairs for their own movies. He designed this rocking chair from *My Uncle* in 1958. —*Page 147*

The director's chair is an archetype, known in the sixteenth century as the X-frame or Savonarola chair. Its folding design made it practical for officers on the battlefield. The director's chair became widely popular after 1892, when the Gold Medal Camp Furniture company presented a commercial model at the Chicago World's Fair. It became a fixture on film sets for the same reasons: it's portable, hard-wearing, and can be customized to make sure everyone knows that the person who sits there is in charge.

The furniture created by Charles and Ray Eames appears in a long list of movies and is a favorite with many Hollywood directors, on and off the set. Steven Spielberg remembers doing his homework on an Eames chair when he was a child, and Billy Wilder was able to enjoy pieces made especially for him, like the Eames Chaise, designed in 1968 so he could take catnaps at work.

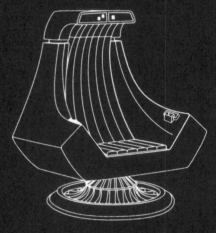

H. R. Giger (1940–2014) was a Swiss artist and sculptor who has gone down in movie history as the creator of one of the silver screen's most unforgettable creatures: Alien, the eighth passenger in Ridley Scott's famous 1979 film. Giger also designed some of the sets for it, which won him an Academy Award for Best Visual Effects. His work can be seen in other films, such as *Poltergeist ii*, *Species*, and *Prometheus*. In 1995 he was asked to design the "batmobile" for *Batman Forever*, but in the end the producer decided not to use it. —Page 145

The Harkonnen chairs never made it to the big screen, either. They were created between 1973 and 1976 for the film *Dune*, which Alejandro Jodorowsky was originally supposed to direct. Salvador Dali, who also had a role in that thwarted production, recommended Giger for the job.

In science fiction movies, art directors tend to design fantastic chairs, like the seats of the Jedi council—a different one for each member—in the *Star Wars* saga created by George Lucas, which premiered in 1977. And on the dark side, we find the throne of Emperor Palpatine. Over the years, they've become furniture of a vintage future.

 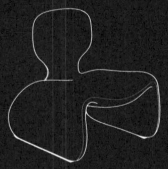  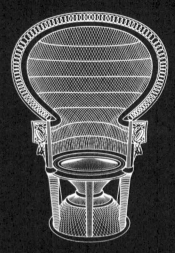 

Films props often include chairs and other pieces of furniture that are available on the market. Some were already famous before they appeared in movies, while others became popular thanks to the silver screen. These are just a few examples.

The Acapulco chair is an anonymous design from the 1950s that appeared alongside Elvis Presley and Ursula Andress in *Fun in Acapulco*, which premiered in 1963.

The Pop style of the Djinn chair (1965) designed by Olivier Mourgue added a splash of color to the white interiors of *2001: A Space Odyssey*, directed by Stanley Kubrick in 1968.

Several of Thonet's No. 18 chairs (1876) accompanied Liza Minnelli in one of the most famous scenes from *Cabaret*, choreographed by Bob Fosse in 1972.

The image of Emmanuelle as an erotic legend will forever be associated with the wicker or rattan chair in which she always appeared in her films. The first was shot by Just Jaeckin in 1974.

Steen Ostergaard's retro-futuristic Cantilever 291 chair (1965) was used in *The Spy Who Loved Me*, the 1977 James Bond film starring Roger Moore and directed by Lewis Gilbert.

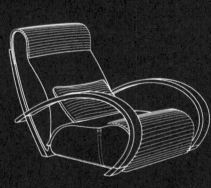   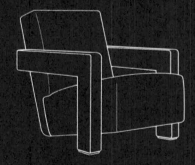

The Casablanca chair (1987) designed by Jaime Tresserra was part of the furniture seen in Kim Basinger's apartment in Tim Burton's 1989 remake of *Batman*.

The Ovalia Egg chair (1968) designed by Henrik Thor-Larsen is featured alongside Tommy Lee Jones and Will Smith on the poster of *Men in Black II*, filmed by Barry Sonnenfeld in 2002.

The Ribbon F582 chair (1966), designed by Pierre Paulin, appeared in the first *Star Trek* series and in the 2017 film *Blade Runner 2049*, directed by Denis Villeneuve.

The 637 Utrecht armchair (1937), designed by Gerrit Thomas Rietveld, was part of the set that Antxón Gómez created for *Pain and Glory*, the Pedro Almodóvar film released in 2019.

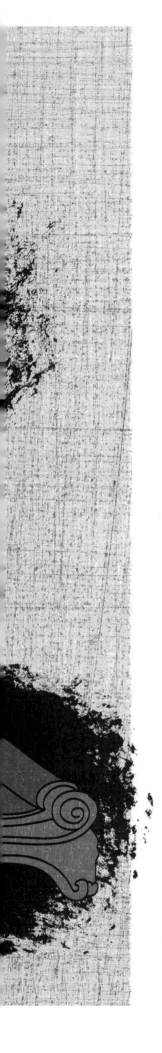

The *Siège d'amour* "Designed" by Edward VII

By Ramón Úbeda

The bedroom scandals of the current British royal family pale in comparison to the hushed-up escapades of the young prince who later became Edward VII, King of Great Britain and Ireland, son of Queen Victoria and Prince Albert. But when he came to the throne in the early twentieth century, at age sixty, his virtues as a diplomat and statesman soon made people forget the sins of his youth. Even so, no history of love furniture would be complete without mentioning Edward's contribution to erotic fantasy in the field of design, for his *Siège d'amour* or "Love Chair," a specimen of which can still be seen in the "Edward VII Room" of the Parisian establishment known as Le Chabanais, deserves a chapter to itself. The young prince commissioned it from a cabinetmaker, as he wanted a piece of furniture that would allow him to frolic with two women at once. The solution to this tricky problem looks more like a gynecological examination table than a love nest. It consists of a padded armchair with metal stirrups and handgrips, mounted on top of an identically upholstered surface with two footrests. What the chronicles don't tell us is if the English playboy achieved the ecstasy he sought or simply came within an inch of cracking his head open on the structure of his padded love seat.

This is an excerpt from a text by Màrius Carol, originally published as an article in issue 33 of *ARDI* magazine, titled "El diseño del amor," and reprinted some years later in the book *Sex Design* (2004), which also featured the Bala Studio chairs. If they'd lived in the nineteenth century, the studio's two members, Xanath Lammoglia and Andrés Amaya, would undoubtedly have been the favorite designers at the court of Edward VII, the Prince of Wales—and later King of Great Britain—with penchant for furniture that could fulfill his erotic fantasies. With such a long and noble history, it seems almost inconceivable that a specialized branch of design hasn't already emerged to cater to this fetish.

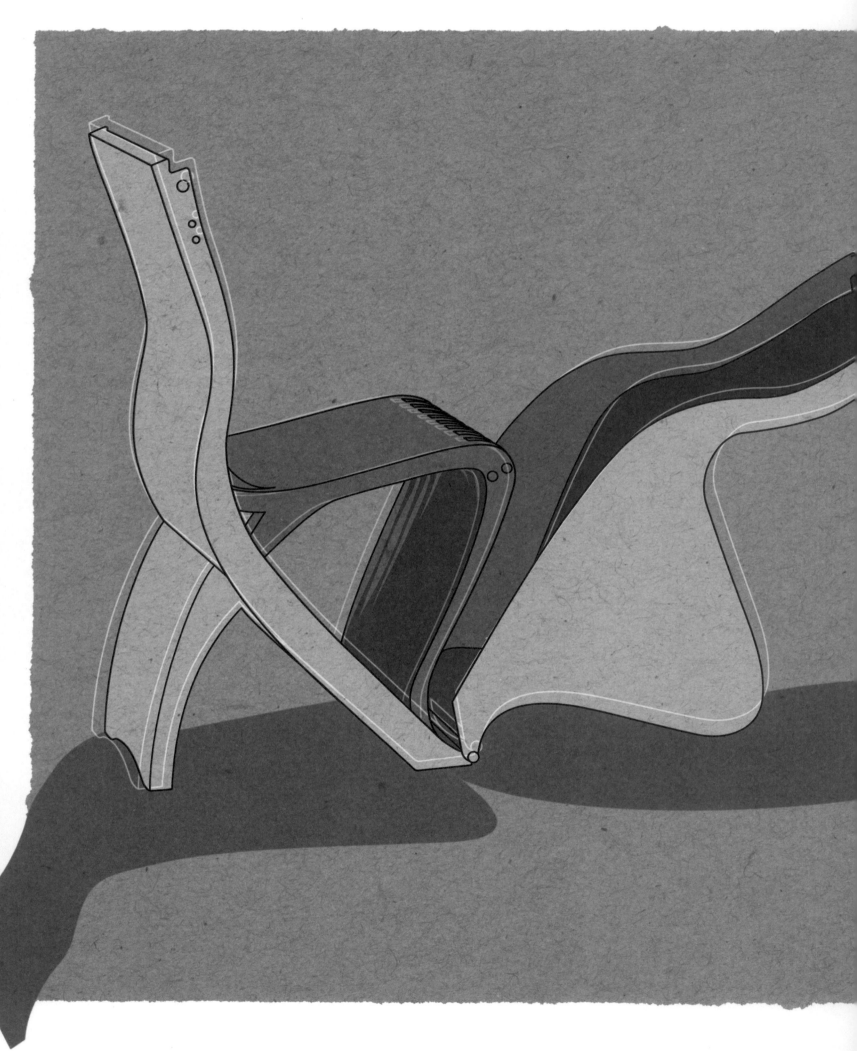

Comfort Is an Illusion

By Ana Domínguez

Many years ago, in the early 1990s, I visited Ron Arad's studio in Camden Town, London, where he eagerly showed me a chair he had just designed and recently finished. And the Rabbit Speaks, as he called it, was a large wooden box with a curving seat shape that opened like a violin case to reveal another chair inside, with the same silhouette as the box. The idea, as he explained it to me, was this: because chairs are shipped inside protective wooden crates, and when they reach their destination, people use those same shipping crates to sit on, why not just give them crates already shaped like chairs?

I thought then, and I still do, that it was a brilliant, completely intriguing idea. I only had one objection: the chair in question would be hard and uncomfortable. When I pointed this out, Ron told me something that's stuck with me for the rest of my career: "Don't be silly. The idea of comfort is an illusion! If you're sitting at a restaurant, and you've got good company and a delicious plate of spaghetti in front of you, you don't care if the chair you're sitting on is comfortable or not, you don't even think about it." Many chairs and many plates of spaghetti have crossed my path since then, unfortunately not always with such auspicious results.

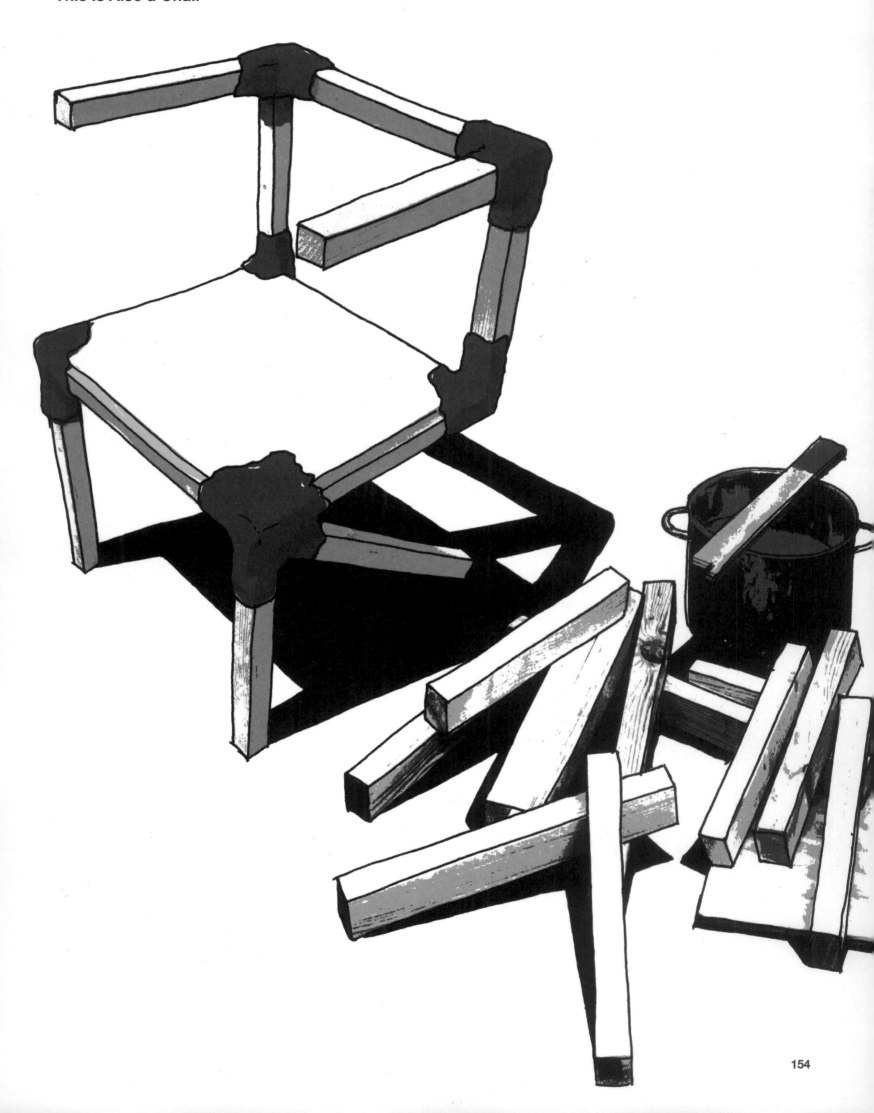

This Is Also a Chair

Amateur Workshop

By Ana Domínguez

Jerszy Seymour has always enjoyed playing the part of *enfant terrible*. I remember when he presented a series of objects at the Vitra Museum, made of a biodegradable plastic derived from potatoes that he had chosen to work by hand rather than industrially—as one would expect with plastic—as a kind of reflection on low-tech and DIY methods. That was a signature Seymour bid for attention. Just when you feel like you've grasped how he thinks, he does something provocative that throws you for a loop. That's why his work operates on a conceptual level, closer to artistic speculation than industry.

His Workshop chair—part of a collection of conceptual creations grouped under the name of Amateur—consists of wood pieces held together, not by nails or other joining systems, but by coarse, shapeless lumps of wax. The chair is one of a series of experiments conducted by Seymour to explore the possibility of a utopian "amateur" society, where wax is a building material as well as a metaphor for the creative energy he believes all human beings possess. Despite its rickety appearance, this is a robust chair that anyone could build, and certainly repair. It's 100% biodegradable and, for the sake of diversification, can be purchased with red, brown, or gray wax. Color is the only concession to aesthetics; the rest is merely the consequence of the assembly method and chosen material, because the only interesting, necessary, indispensable thing here is the idea. Everything else is incidental.

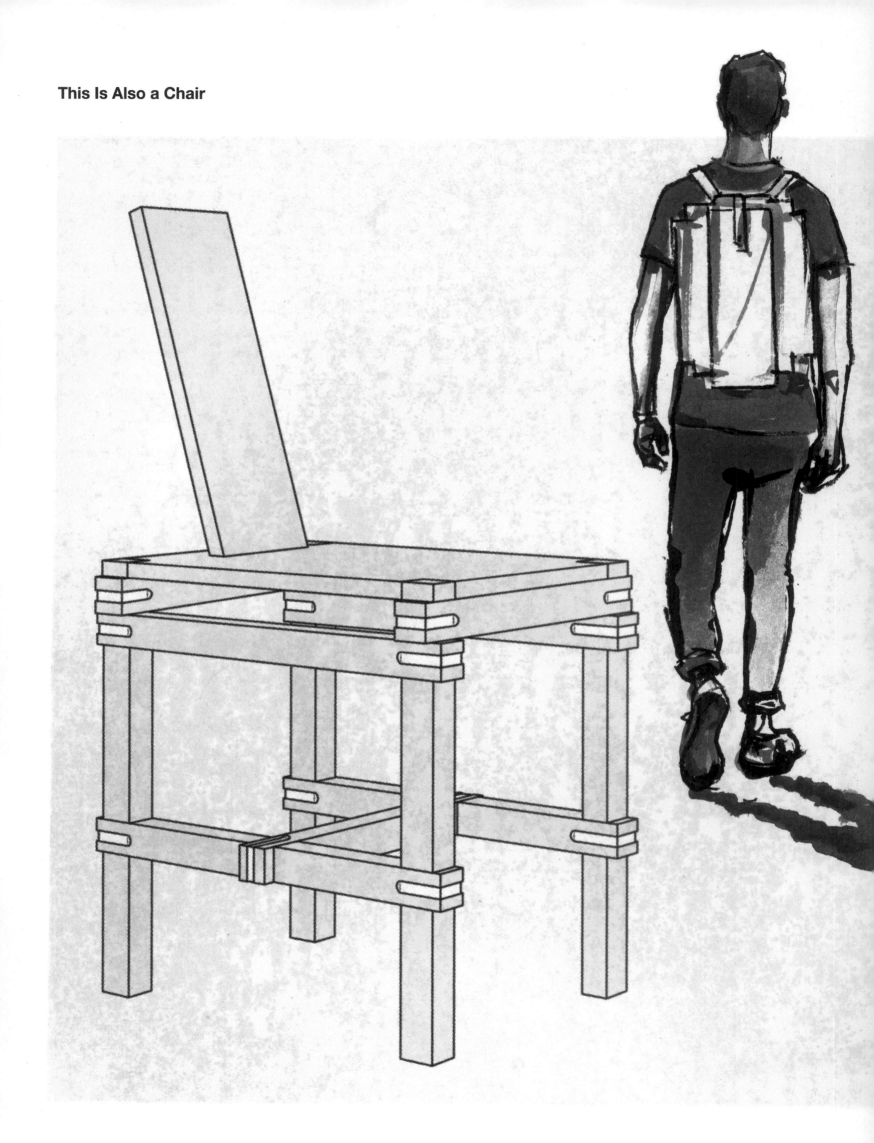

Luxury in a Backpack

By Ana Domínguez

The Nomadic is an ephemeral seat with a wandering soul that has a fascinating effect: it seems to trigger a small cultural short-circuit in your brain. On the one hand, you're attracted to the idea of a chair that can be taken apart and the nifty carrying solution; it's a portable chair in backpack form that can be assembled without nails or hammers. But on the other, it seems inconvenient to lug around a chair that's neither light nor practical nor necessarily easy to assemble, even though the designer claims it only takes two minutes. Basically, it's everything you wouldn't want in a chair to take on a hike or camping trip, especially in this age of sophisticated materials and technological revolution.

Nevertheless, you can't help loving it, because what makes it appealing isn't its practicality but its message. It makes a statement about the contemporary world, the rat race, the harried lifestyle where time has become a luxury. It reminds us that this luxury has nothing do to with material things and everything to do with experience, that moment we choose to devote to a task and give ourselves a time-out, a personal break. In that context, comfort is neither present nor expected—at least no more than you might hope to find by sitting on a random boulder.

A Readymade Seat

By Isabel del Río

Can anything be turned into a seat? If we accept that a seat is any place, object, or piece of furniture on which we rest our backsides for the purpose of sitting, then the answer is yes.

Ever since Marcel Duchamp came along with his *objets trouvés* or readymades—existing objects transformed to give them a brand-new meaning—anything is possible. The French artist opened the floodgates. However, with the advent of semiotics theories (which study signs and symbols as tools of cultural communication) and the postmodern movement, people began to believe that objects were imbued with symbolic meaning and users could therefore establish psychological relationships with them.

That's how German designer Frank Schreiner, founder of Stiletto Studios, came up with his comical recipe for turning a plain shopping cart into a chair. And no, I'm not talking about that tiny fold-out space on grocery carts where kids can sit while their parents shop. I'm talking about a limited-edition chair that's ended up in museum collections, for two fundamental reasons. One is the transformation of its cultural status, from ordinary object to unique object. And the other is its ironic message: a supermarket shopping cart becomes a symbol of the voracious consumerism of a liberal economy.

So how did the designer do it? He took a shopping cart, opened up the front so the sitter's legs could hang down, bent the upper part of the sides outward to serve as armrests, and covered the seat and back with transparent plastic to ensure at least a modicum of comfort. Conclusion: if you dig deep enough, there's a seat inside every object.

This Is Also a Chair

A Chair To Last a Lifetime

By Isabel del Río

Enrique and his daughter Sara were strolling through the well-known Gràcia district in the city of Barcelona. Sara was five years old. In a few weeks she would turn six. She was growing up so quickly. She exhibited the fresh spontaneity typical of her age and an insatiable curiosity about everything. Enrique and Sara had a habit of walking the same route two or three times a week. But that day Sara, in one of those impetuous flashes her father loved so much, wanted to go a different way. And so it was that, while strolling down Carrer Verdi, they both noticed a different facade on the left side of the street. It was a building in the Catalan Modernist style, with a lovely wooden door flanked by two windows. Both the door and windows had carved lintels with plant motifs, and the window grilles looked to be made of wrought iron. The door stood wide open, and an acrylic sign by the entrance read H20. Father and daughter unanimously decided to enter.

Once inside, they discovered a diaphanous space, all painted white and very brightly lit. The owner explained that it was a contemporary art gallery specialized in architecture, design, and photography. Just then Sara spied a yellow chair with a striking back and a seat so low she assumed it must be made for children, and promptly sat down on it. As he watched her, Enrique asked the owner and producer of the seat why he had a child's chair in an art gallery. Joaquim Ruiz Millet, as the owner was called, explained that it was the work of a young Catalan designer named Martí Guixé, and that it was more than a child's chair. It was a conceptual proposal, as the author intended it to be chair that would last a lifetime.

"A lifetime?" Enrique echoed, puzzled.

"Yes," Joaquim replied. "It's a living chair! You'll never need another, because it grows with the child. You just have to keep stacking books on the seat, adjusting it to the child's height."

Enrique thought it would make a wonderfully timeless gift for his Sara. And ever since, every year on St. George's Day, he has given his daughter a new book to place on the seat once she's finished it, symbolizing the stages of Sara's journey toward both physical and intellectual maturity.

This Is Also a Chair

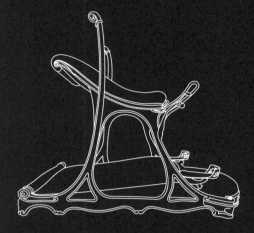

The *Siège d'amour*, "designed" by Edward VII so he could cavort with two ladies at once, dates from 1890. —*Page 151*

Sex furniture is not a contemporary design specialty, except for one pair of Mexican designers, Xanath Lammoglia and Andrés Amaya, who have set out to fill that market niche and come up with a chair for each type of sexual practice.

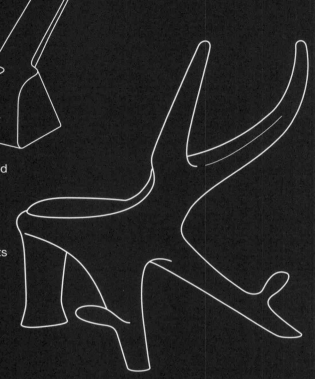

Barbarella (2003) is specifically designed for cunnilingus. Fellatio (2004) has an unambiguous name and shape.

Another more recent example of their work is Adela, a seat with gripping posts that make it ideal for straddling one's partner and "riding in style."

Jerszy Seymour was born in Berlin in 1968 to a Canadian mother and German father who were both ballet dancers. He grew up in London, home to the Royal College of Art, which trains designers with an artistic bent—or vice versa. Jerszy clearly belongs to the category of artists who want to learn the fundamentals of design in order to subvert them. His work is conceptual and premeditatedly anti-aesthetic, which explains how he became the co-founder and director of the Dirty Art Department at the Sandberg Instituut in Amsterdam. His pieces, like the Workshop chair, can be found in the collections of the MoMA, New York, and the Centre Pompidou, Paris. —*Page 155*

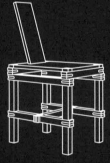 

Jorge Penadés is not and probably never will be a chair designer. He works the less commercial angle of the design business, coming up with experimental ideas with the aim of transforming the industry. He designed the Nomadic chair in 2013 as his senior project—a graduation requirement at the Escola Superior de Disseny i d'Arts Plástiques (ESDAP) in Barcelona—and as an announcement of what he believed the future of the profession would be: radical, rational, and sustainable. —*Page 157*

Ron Arad has been an *enfant terrible* of design since he appeared on the scene in the 1980s. Spanish audiences were introduced to him in an article published by *ARDI* magazine, titled "El bruto más fino del mundo" [The World's Most Refined Brute], where we saw his iconic Rover chair, made from the seat of a Rover vehicle. He had made it in his workshop before he turned thirty. Over the course of his career, Arad has made many more chairs, hammering out limited editions or working on commissions for firms like Vitra and Moroso. Products for industry that all started out as experimental concepts, like the one that inspired his 1994 creation And the Rabbit Speaks. —*Page 153*

Consumer's Rest is the name that Frank Schreiner, a member of the Berlin-based Stiletto Studios, gave to the grocery cart he turned into a manifesto-chair in 1983. Around one hundred of these chairs were made, half of them with a gold finish to further emphasize the anti-consumerist message. —*Page 159*

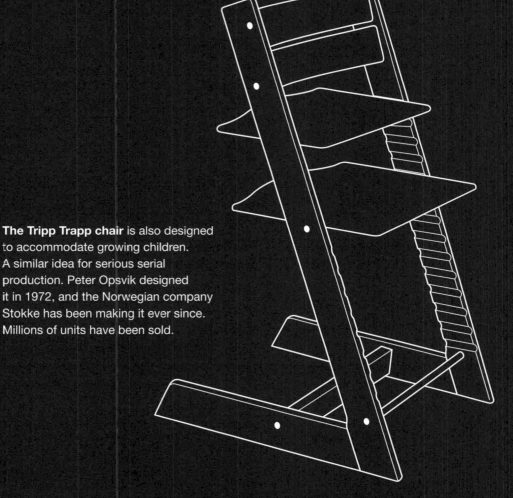

Martí Guixé divides his time between Barcelona and Berlin. He's used a variety of titles on his business cards: Technogastrosopher, Tapa-ist, MultiTalent, and, lately, Ex-designer, which is what he prefers to be called now, although his internationally acknowledged talent continues to defy classification. Guixé can be described as a designer who doesn't design: if someone asks for a chair, he'll offer them an idea for sitting. This one is called H2O, after the gallery that commissioned it. It comes in white, black, red, yellow, or orange painted fiberglass. —*Page 161*

The Tripp Trapp chair is also designed to accommodate growing children. A similar idea for serious serial production. Peter Opsvik designed it in 1972, and the Norwegian company Stokke has been making it ever since. Millions of units have been sold.

Art or Design?

By Rosina Gómez-Baeza

> The art of a chair is not its resemblance to art, but is partly its reasonableness, usefulness and scale as a chair. These are proportion, which is visible reasonableness. The art in art is partly the assertion of someone's interest regardless of other considerations. A work of art exists as itself; a chair exists as a chair itself. And the idea of a chair isn't a chair.
>
> Donald Judd (1986)

In the early 1960s, a radical movement emerged in New York and took a stand against objectual art, against the dematerialization of art. Rauschenberg and Kienholz, as well as the Pop artists, had followed the trail blazed by Duchamp and his *objets trouvés*, experimenting and exploring the recovery of discarded objects and even trash. This incipient, intensely rigorous movement was minimalism. Judd was one of its greatest champions, defending three-dimensionality, clean and simple forms, and the absence of all symbolic or intellectual references. Initially, this hitherto unheard-of art was fittingly referred to as ABC Art or Primary Structures. Both names explained the meaning of this art form, but in 1965 the philosopher Richard Wollheim coined the term minimal art, which stuck and is still used today. Though many critics likened it to Russian Constructivism, this no-frills, accessible art was intentionally American, promoting an intense individual experience through the interaction of object, space, and spectator. An art in search of harmony. In 1967, another philosopher, Roland Barthes, announced the death of the author and the birth of the reader/interpreter, in consonance with Duchamp's dictum that the spectator must be the sole interpreter of the work.

Knowing all this, it's no wonder that Donald Judd—always concerned with execution, the completion of his pieces—found himself drawn to furniture design. It happened in the early 1970s. First, he devised a wooden bed and a metal sink for 101 Spring Street, his studio and residence and current headquarters of the Judd Foundation. In 1977 he designed more furniture for his house in Marfa, Texas. The children's bedrooms and the other rooms needed tables, desks, beds, benches, chairs... In 1984 he organized an exhibition of his metal furniture at what was then Max Protetch's art and architecture gallery in New York. After that, Judd's interest in design grew, and he began to study, theorize, and write about this discipline. He also got involved in producing and even distributing his creations. From 1984 to 1993, he continued to design and control the quality of the pieces, whether they were manufactured industrially or by artisans, insisting on skilled workmanship in both cases.

"And the idea of a chair isn't a chair," Judd said. Does this mean that Donald Judd's chair is a work of art, another creation from the grand master of minimalism? How should we interpret this statement?

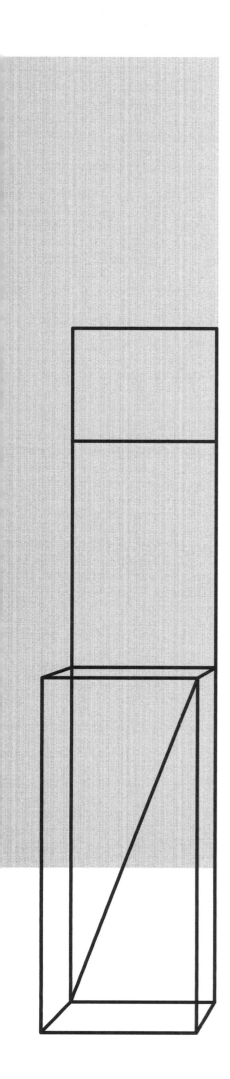

Robert Wilson

By Rosina Gómez-Baeza

Born in Texas in 1941, Robert Wilson is the ultimate creator, a multifaceted, prolific "maker" universally acknowledged as a master in each of his artistic fields. He has designed a vast number of chairs in response to the need created by a ground-breaking fiction that burst onto stages around the world with all the force of the absolute work. He turns his chairs into performing objects. Actor and object become sculptures that speak of transcendence. He gives chairs—the elements most often caressed by this miracle worker of the stage and the visual arts—the same importance as actors, sound, and lighting, all key elements in his productions.

As a visual artist, he knows and references the great artists of his time. The lightness and subtly geometric representations of Cézanne, the French Postimpressionist painter, have inspired Wilson, and that influence is patent in many of his pieces: the Curie, the Einstein, the Elsa chair, the Bamboo chair, and the Alice in Bed chair, to name but a few. He has hearkened to the call of other great masters: the Mondrian chair revolves around this Dutch artist's abstraction. Through the shapes and materials of his chairs, Wilson also alludes to other individuals who inspire him (as with his two Queen Victoria chairs, in intimate conversation with... Prince Albert, perhaps?).

What interests me most about Wilson's chairs is the quest for abstraction, for simplicity, the intrinsic quality conferred by their very nature. I also like that they never lose their close connection to space, to the other, key elements in Wilson's artistic conceptions. He sees the chair as part of a whole—a whole which, by way of fiction, comes close to the truth.

Dalí's Leda-Armchair Sculpture

By Marisa García Vergara

Dalí's first experiment with a chair led him to invent surrealist objects.

Determined to alter ordinary household items and create irrational objects with symbolic function, Dalí naturally began with a chair. In his *Secret Life*, Dalí told how one day his friend Jean-Michel Frank, the Parisian decorator, gave him two chairs "in the purest 1900 style," to which he immediately made a series of changes, such as trading the leather seat for one made of chocolate, or screwing a golden Louis xv doorknob under one of the feet to extend it and make the piece so unstable that a heavy tread or bang of the door would be enough to make the chair topple over. He also decided that one leg should stand in a glass of beer, which would spill each time the chair keeled over. "I called this dreadfully uncomfortable chair, which produced a profound uneasiness in all who saw it, the 'atmospheric chair'," Dalí wrote. With it, he had "invented objects which one never knew where to put (every place one chooses immediately appearing unsatisfactory), intended to create anxieties that would cease only the moment one got rid of them."

After his first encounter with Frank at the home of the Vicomte de Noailles in 1930, Dalí continued drawing furniture and all sorts of decorative objects, from faucets and knobs to others whose use is less clear, to be manufactured by Chanaux & Co., where Frank was the artistic director. However, few of them were actually produced—no doubt because Frank had a reputation to maintain. Years later, the firm BD Barcelona, with Oscar Tusquets at the helm, would produce some of them, including the Leda chair, based on the 1935 Dalí painting *Femme à la tête rose* and materialized by the sculptor Joaquim Camps.

The Leda chair does not keel over, as the brass frame is far heavier than the slender lines of its anthropomorphic design would suggest. Nor does it seem to respect Dalí's maxim that a chair can even be used for sitting, but only on the condition that one sits uncomfortably. However, it does fulfill Dalí's prophecy: "It was my contention that these objects would have a great commercial success, for everyone underestimated the unconscious masochistic buyer who was avidly looking for the object capable of making him suffer in the most indefinite and least obvious way."

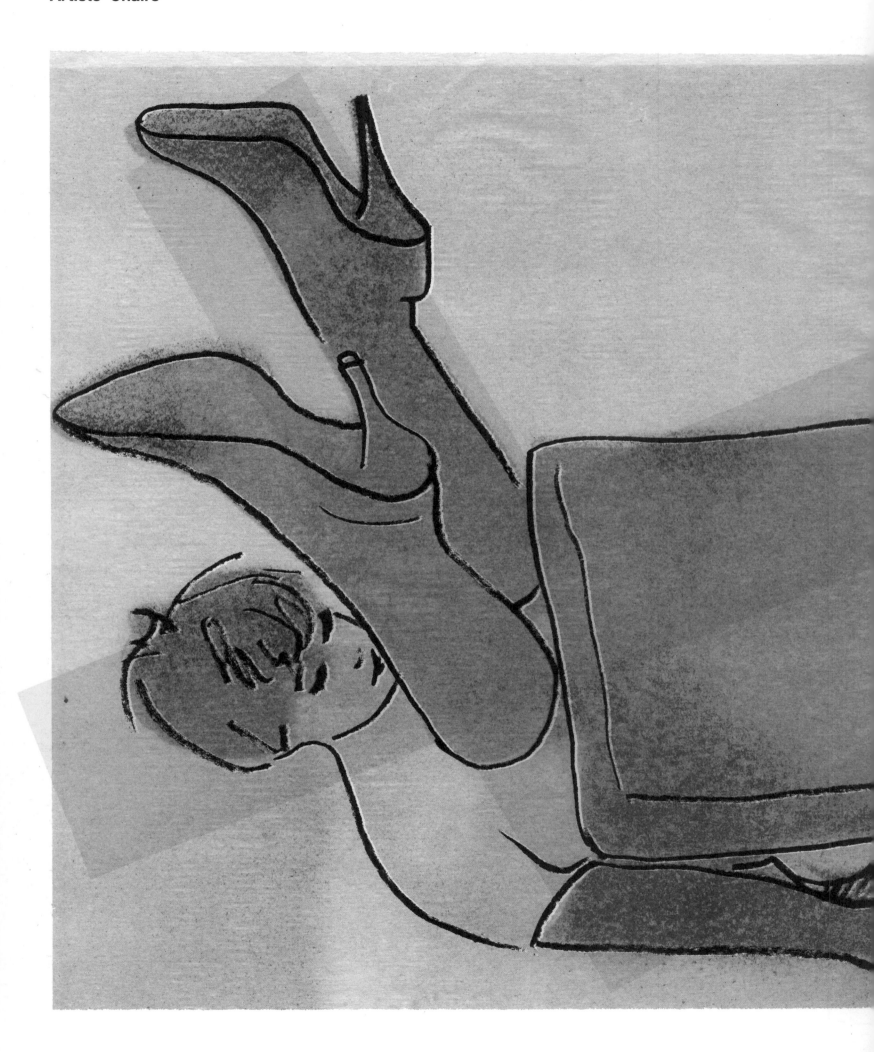

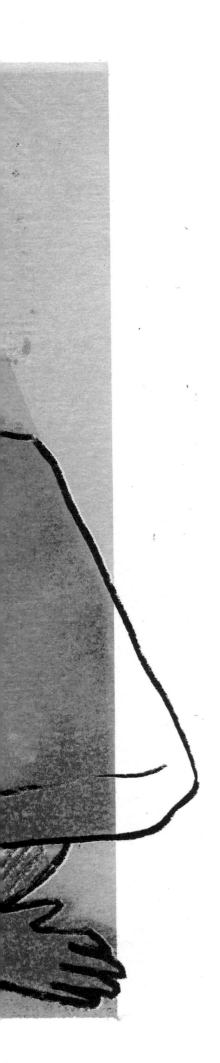

Allen Jones's "Living Room"

By Ramón Úbeda

British artist Allen Jones had no compunctions about literally turning women into furniture. The year was 1969, the end of a decade marked by the artistic and sexual revolutions. The time was ripe for bold, controversial ideas, and Allen must have thought he could participate in both revolutions at once. He embraced Pop art, along with fellow British artists like David Hockney—American Pop was dominated by Andy Warhol—and surprised friends and strangers alike with a project featuring a collection of furniture which, though quite serviceable, was not to everyone's taste. His furniture sculptures—chair, tables, and hatstand—made from female mannequins, half naked or sporting latex and a BDSM look, had one foot in the art world and, given their functionality, the other in design, but they ended up being classified as art, probably because no manufacturer dared to mass-produce them.

A Chair of Eternal Rest

By Isabel Campi

It's hard to imagine how a chair can poetically evoke death. We shudder at the sight of the electric chair because of its cold functionality; it's no coincidence that Andy Warhol devoted an entire series of screenprints to this sinister icon of American culture.

The electric chair is a product of heartless technical engineering, whereas the Golgotha chair designed by Gaetano Pesce in 1972 is an object halfway between sculpture and design, remarkable not for its functional and productive qualities but for its problematic materiality and thought-provoking presence.

It falls under the heading of what the architect, editor, and design critic Alessandro Mendini called "objects for spiritual use" in the early 1970s: furniture as a critical tool that offers a visual interpretation of interior design at the outer limits of practicality.

The Golgotha chairs are part of a collection of objects inspired by the Bible, and more specifically the Passion of Christ, explicitly alluding to the theme of sacrifice. They are made one by one from a fiberglass cloth containing Dacron Fiberfill. This fabric is stiffened in a bath of polyester resin, hung on wire hooks, and draped into the form of a chair, making each piece unique and inimitable.

When we see this chair, we can't tell if we're looking at a new object or an old one, an industrial product or an archeological find, because each is totally imperfect, suggesting wear-and-tear and the passage of time. In postmodern terms, we might call these chairs "future ruins." Part burial cloth and part furniture, these stiff white shrouds remind us that life is fleeting and, inevitably, one day our own mortal remains will be wrapped in one of them, on the way to our eternal rest.

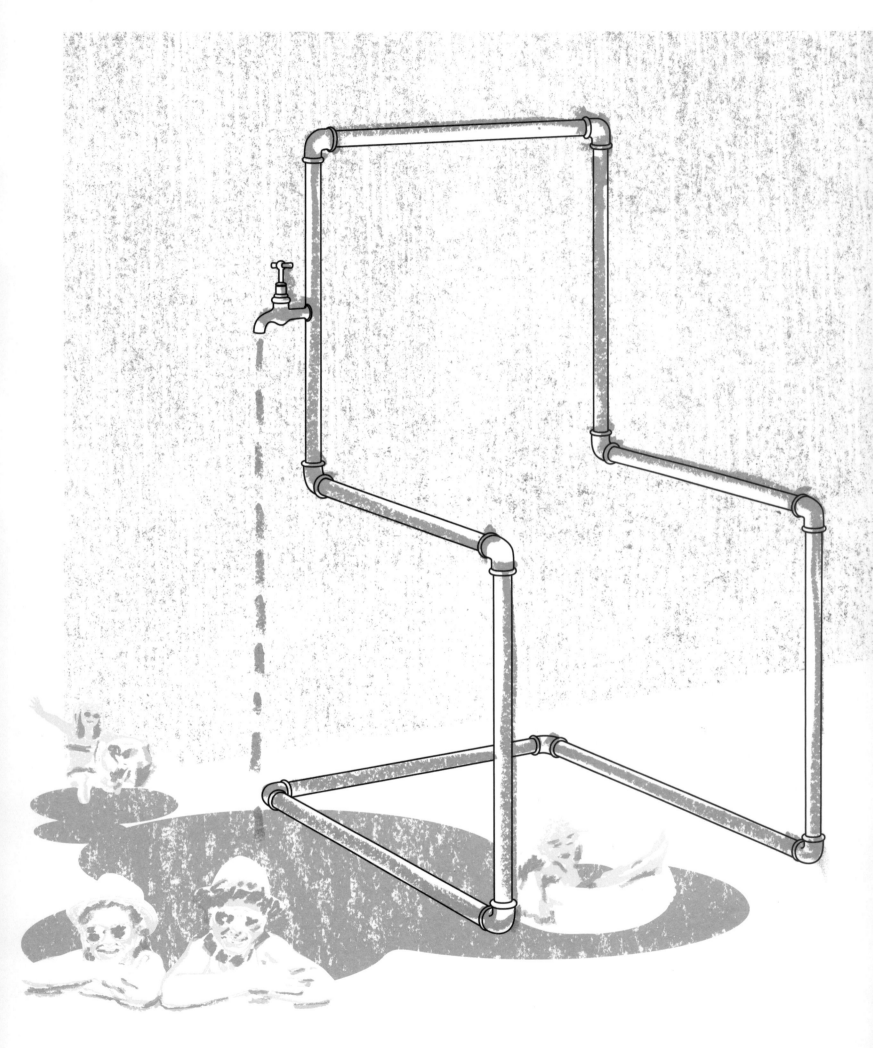

"La suor de la cadira"

By Rosina Gómez-Baeza

This sculpture could be classified as belonging to the Dada movement that Duchamp launched with his legendary *Fountain* in 1917. Brossa was part of that disruptive tendency, in which the artist ignored or deliberately avoided what had long been considered the inherent functions of art—in other words, narrative and aesthetic. The language of this new, avant-garde artistic expression—we can also place objectual and conceptual art under this heading—was quite different, but it had a universal quality and has endured to the present day. Above all, it represented rebellion, irreverence, and even destruction. Yet Brossa was freedom, poetry, individuality...

It's hard for a designer to calculate the resistance of the contraption called a chair. Brossa gave his "version" of this contraption a human quality—the chair sweats—as well as an ironic function, incorporating a faucet to drain the perspiration. I'm not sure why, but this object-poem reminds me of the characters from *Alice in Wonderland*, that delightful fantasy where nothing is what it seems. *La cadira* is an endearing fiction, but it's also a work of art that will make us smile and give us pleasure for centuries to come.

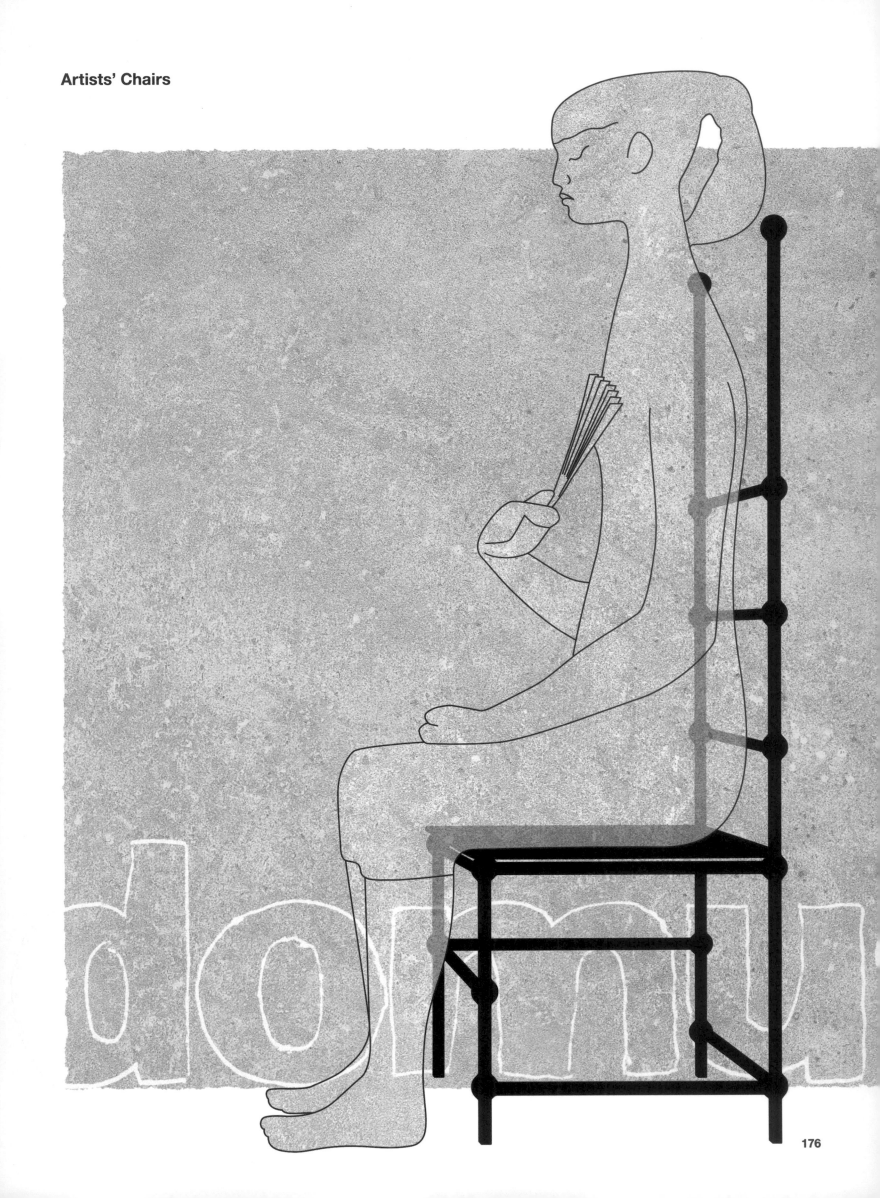

The Sánchez Chair

By Ana Domínguez

Spanish sculptor José Luis Sánchez had saved a pair of overalls given to him on a trip to Finland by Pi, Timo Sarpaneva's first wife, who owned a company that designed work clothes. He had met Timo and Tapio Wirkkala years earlier at the 1954 Triennale di Milano, when José Luis was a young intern assigned to look after the Spanish pavilion designed by Ramón Vázquez Molezún, while Sarpaneva was the main attraction at his own country's pavilion. That time in Milan proved quite productive for José Luis, who—by way of supporting Tita, Gio Ponti's daughter, in her romantic designs on the handsome Molezún—frequented the great architect's studio/residence, which was also the headquarters of *Domus* magazine at the time.

Back home in Madrid, José Luis continued to work on his sculptures, many of which were associated with buildings designed by the great architects of his day, like Antonio Lamela and Miguel Fisac. For one of those sculptures, a seated Madonna, Sánchez designed a chair, a geometric structure made of iron. Extremely simple, solid, and almost archetypal in its minimalism, the chair promised to be unbearably uncomfortable for any backside not made of stone. One day the telephone rang: it was his friend Tita, calling to ask if he had happened to design any chairs worth publishing. Without a second thought, José Luis sent her a photo of that chair made for his stone sculpture, and shortly afterwards the "Sánchez chair" appeared in *Domus.* As he mischievously confessed to me, it was the only time that magazine ever published anything of his.

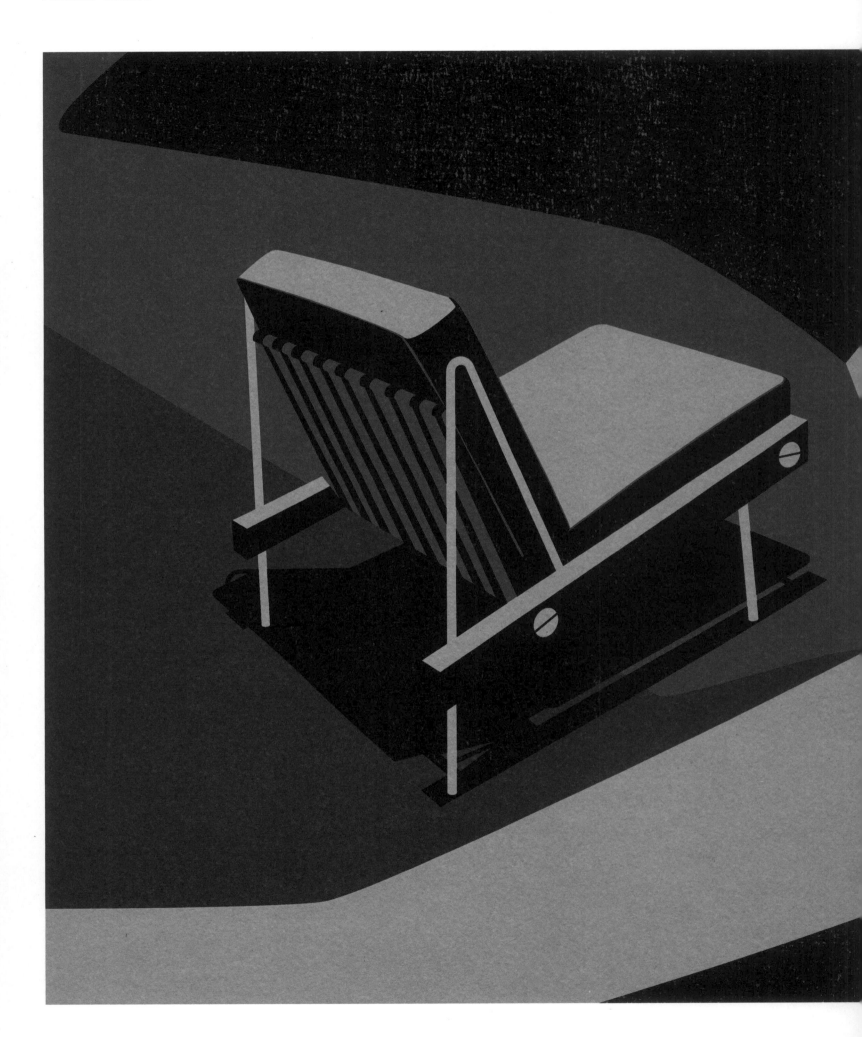

A "Team" Effort

By Rosalía Torrent

A lot of things happened in Spain in 1957. Actually, things were already happening, but that was the year they decided on a name. One group of artists, divided between Paris and Córdoba, christened themselves as Equipo 57 or "Team 57", while another crew in Madrid took the name El Paso. They couldn't have been more different. The Equipo guys turned to lines and planes, while the El Paso contingent resorted to fabrics, cardboards, and signic brushwork (though in Paris it was actually the members of Equipo 57 who survived with the brush). But they had two things in common: the language of the avant-garde, and their opposition to the Franco dictatorship. Thanks to them, the art world, then painfully thin, began to put on weight—and to testify.

Art was expanding, but what about design? Was anyone in Spain even practicing design at the time? A few, yes, and our "team" (who also made art) was among them. They made chairs, for one thing. And, of course, the first chair could only be called Córdoba. Although the group was born in a Parisian café, when they returned to Spain they headed for the city that three of the group's five members—Juan Cuenca, Juan Serrano, and José Duarte—called home. Ángel Duarte (not José's brother) had been born in Cáceres, and Agustín Ibarrola in Bilbao. Did I say five? There were more, for others came and went from the group, but those five established the core of shared friendship and tastes. They worked together, rented together, and soon parted ways.

But they had time to accomplish quite a lot—time, for instance, to create the Córdoba chair. Notice how solid it is, yet how light. The holm oak timbers that form the side braces are echoes of the cartwright who lived next door. They're spokes from his wheels. The heads of two gigantic screws hold them firmly in place. Nothing to hide. Everything in plain sight. Slenderness in the metal rods of the legs. The seat reclines on that idea solidified by the Bauhaus. The leg is extended at just the right angle. Light cushioning. The collapsible structure makes it easy to move: the same idea popularized by Ikea and anticipated by Thonet's No. 14. The young Darro firm—even younger than the "team," having been founded in 1958—saw this feature as its greatest strength and began to produce the chair. It was ideal for export. The manufacturer also had a showroom in Madrid on Calle Lista, a street later renamed in honor of the philosopher Ortega y Gasset. With its sights set on northern Europe, Darro came across this southern group and saw in their work the simplicity it sought, the perfect element. The piece was picked up by the legendary magazine *Muebles y Decoración*. The future had begun.

Hexaphonic Diaphragm Chair 30, opus 11

By Ramón Úbeda

José María Cruz Novillo belongs to the most important generation of designers in the history of Spain, designers who created its modern image and prepared the way for all those who would come after them. He drew the Spanish Socialist Party (PSOE) brand, defined the Repsol logo and the colors of its gas stations, created the symbols of the Spanish Railway Company (RENFE) and the National Treasury (Tesoro Público), and even designed the peseta bills we all used before the euro arrived. For a time, he and others like Alberto Corazón and Carlos Rolando were responsible for designing the visual identity of Spain's leading institutions and corporations. They will always be remembered as pioneers of a profession that has changed dramatically over the years. In the digital age, designers can achieve wonders, but guys like them are inimitable. The two who worked in Madrid had more in common than their choice of occupation: they also led a double life as established artists, each in his own style.

And Cruz Novillo's style is unique. Born in Cuenca the same year the Spanish Civil War began, he has been—in this order—a draftsman, designer, painter, and post-Dada sculptor who works with all sorts of materials, including sounds. In the 1990s he began developing a concept he called "Diaphragm," based on the combination of a variable number of elements or units. He applied it to different works, some of which are also four-dimensional, like *Diafragma hexafónico Chair 46.656* [Hexaphonic Diaphragm Chair 46,656], a sculpture in the form of a chair—or the other way around—that can generate cycles of up to forty-six thousand six hundred and fifty-six unique pieces. In 2007, he produced a pilot edition of thirty pieces with the technical assistance of industrial designer Antonio Serrano. Each chair has six components—a seat, a back, and four legs—which Cruz Novillo uses to create different chromatic and phonic combinations with repetition. The result is a 3-minute, 36-second-long chromophonic composition titled *Diafragma hexafónico Chair 30, opus 11* [Hexaphonic Diaphragm Chair 30, opus 11], for synthesized wind instrument.

But this is nothing in comparison to the artist's latest variation on the same theme, a chronochromophonic work called *Diafragma dodecafónico 8.916.100.448.256, opus 14* [Dodecaphonic Diaphragm 8,916,100,448,256, opus 14], which contains all the permutations with repetition of 12 colors (red, orange, white, magenta, yellow, green, purple, blue, light blue, black, brown, and gray), the 12 notes of the equal-tempered scale, and 12 lengths of time. It would take 3,390,410 years, 31 days, 11 hours, 31 minutes, and 12 seconds to experience them all; if you plan to try, you'd better take a seat.

Artists' Chair

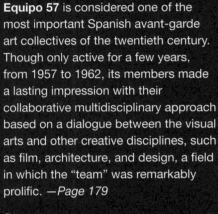

Equipo 57 is considered one of the most important Spanish avant-garde art collectives of the twentieth century. Though only active for a few years, from 1957 to 1962, its members made a lasting impression with their collaborative multidisciplinary approach based on a dialogue between the visual arts and other creative disciplines, such as film, architecture, and design, a field in which the "team" was remarkably prolific. —*Page 179*

Thanks to their collaboration with Darro, the Danona cooperative in Azpeitia, Guipúzcoa, and other manufacturers, quite a few of their seats and chairs hit the market, including the Córdoba (1959), the Erlo (1963), which won the Silver Delta, the one known simply as the Armchair (1962), and a design with a metal frame and wood lathes submitted to a "furniture competition for modest homes" organized by EXCO (Spanish Ministry of Housing) in 1961. Oriol Bohigas sat on the judges' panel.

Darro, founded by Paco Muñoz in 1959, was a pioneering firm which, for a time, was the premier showcase of modernity in the Spanish capital. The company manufactured, displayed, and sold furniture as well as decorative objects, following the standard business model of the day, but it was ahead of its time in its choice of collaborators and the decision to add an art gallery to its furniture showroom.

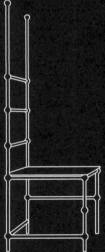

José Luis Sánchez (1926–2018) was a Spanish sculptor, a contemporary of Chillida who pioneered the use of abstraction alongside Rafael Canogar, Antonio Saura, and other leading names of that period. He also had connections to design through his friends and forged ties with architecture thanks to his many collaborations with some of the top professionals working in Madrid in the second half of the twentieth century, including Carvajal, Fernández del Amo, Fisac, and Lamela. This chair is part of a sculpture titled *Muchacha del abanico* [Girl with a Fan], which he created in 1955 for the Directorate-General of Architecture of the Ministry of Public Works and Urban Planning in Madrid. —*Page 177*

Leda is an armchair-sculpture, more like an artwork than a functional piece of furniture. This chair and the Leda table are part of a series of designs made by Salvador Dalí in the 1930s, which were developed, produced, and sold by BD Barcelona Design nearly half a century later. In addition to these two pieces, inspired by the painting *Femme à la tête rose*, in 1991 several more objects appeared: the Bracelli, Cajones, and Muletas lamps, the Dalí Vis-à-Vis de Gala sofa, and the Rinoceróntico door handle, all based on drawings the artist had made in Paris for Jean-Michel Frank, a well-known furniture designer and interior decorator in Dalí's time. —*Page 169*

Hatstand, Table and Chair are the three pieces that comprise Allen Jones's "living room furniture" series from 1969. If they caused a scandal back then, just imagine how modern audiences would react. Jones, the most controversial British artist of his day, chose the path of provocation early on—he was expelled from the Royal College of Art—and his influence was absorbed by fashion and film, two worlds with a higher tolerance for sexually explicit content than the design industry. In his later work, somewhat less provocative, though never innocent and always attention-grabbing, he branched out into a wide range of media, and his efforts were rewarded in 1986 when he was elected to the Royal Academy of Arts, London. —*Page 171*

José María Cruz Novillo began developing his Diaphragms—tetraphonic, pentaphonic, hexaphonic, heptaphonic, and decaphonic—on a variety of surfaces, from canvases to the facade of the National Statistics Institute in Madrid. In 2009 he was inducted into the San Fernando Academy of Fine Arts and gave a performance of *Diafragma heptafónico 49, opus 13* during his acceptance speech. One year later, at the ARCO art fair, he introduced *Diafragma dodecafónico 8.916.100.448.256, opus 14*, a cycle of nearly nine trillion different and unique works that will take almost 34,000 centuries to complete. Until then, its progress can be followed at cruznovilloopus14.com. —*Page 181*

The minimalist furniture of Donald Judd (1928–1994) is still being made today by Lenhi AG, the same Swiss company that began producing it in 1984, and sold through the Judd Foundation. His designs are made of sheet metal painted in RAL colors. Chairs, armchairs, tables, and shelves that often look like sculptures. Or vice versa. —*Page 186*

Robert Wilson is a one-man show. He studied painting in Paris and architecture at the Pratt Institute in New York. His wide-ranging vision has made him a consummate artist, renowned, respected, admired, and capable of painting any stage with light. When it comes to props, he has a special fondness for chairs, which he designs himself, envisioning them as sculptures and treating them as independent characters in his productions. He has brought Einstein and Stalin to the stage, represented in the abstract form of a chair, as well as Queen Victoria in *A Letter from Queen Victoria* (1974) and Mondrian in the opera *De Materie* (1989). —*Page 167*

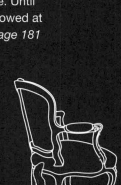

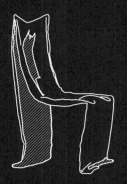

Joan Brossa (1919–1998) created *La suor de la cadira* [Sweat of the Chair] in 1990. This was not the first time he had referred to or incorporated a chair in one of his object-poems: a few years earlier he had presented a work titled *Mutació* [Mutation], a "chair with a tail" that also continued the tradition begun by Marcel Duchamp of taking an object out of context and giving it symbolic value. In this case, the chair with a fox's tail is a metaphor for the gentrification of the art world. —*Page 175*

Brossa was close to other artists, like Miró and Tàpies, who also repeatedly used chairs in their works. Joan Miró created his *Seated Woman and Child* in 1967. Antoni Tàpies produced the covered chairs series (*Chair, Chair with Bar,* and *Covered Chair*) in 1970.

The Golgotha chairs designed by Gaetano Pesce in 1972 bear a strong resemblance to Tàpies's sculpture, with one significant difference: you can actually sit in a Golgotha chair. The Italian architect and designer, born in La Spezia in 1939, has proved in the course of his long career that design can also be approached from an artistic perspective. When he founded Bracciodiferro in the 1970s and participated in the historic MoMA exhibition *Italy: The New Domestic Landscape* in New York City, where he has lived and worked since 1983, people called it "experimental design." These days the proper term is "art design." —*Page 173*

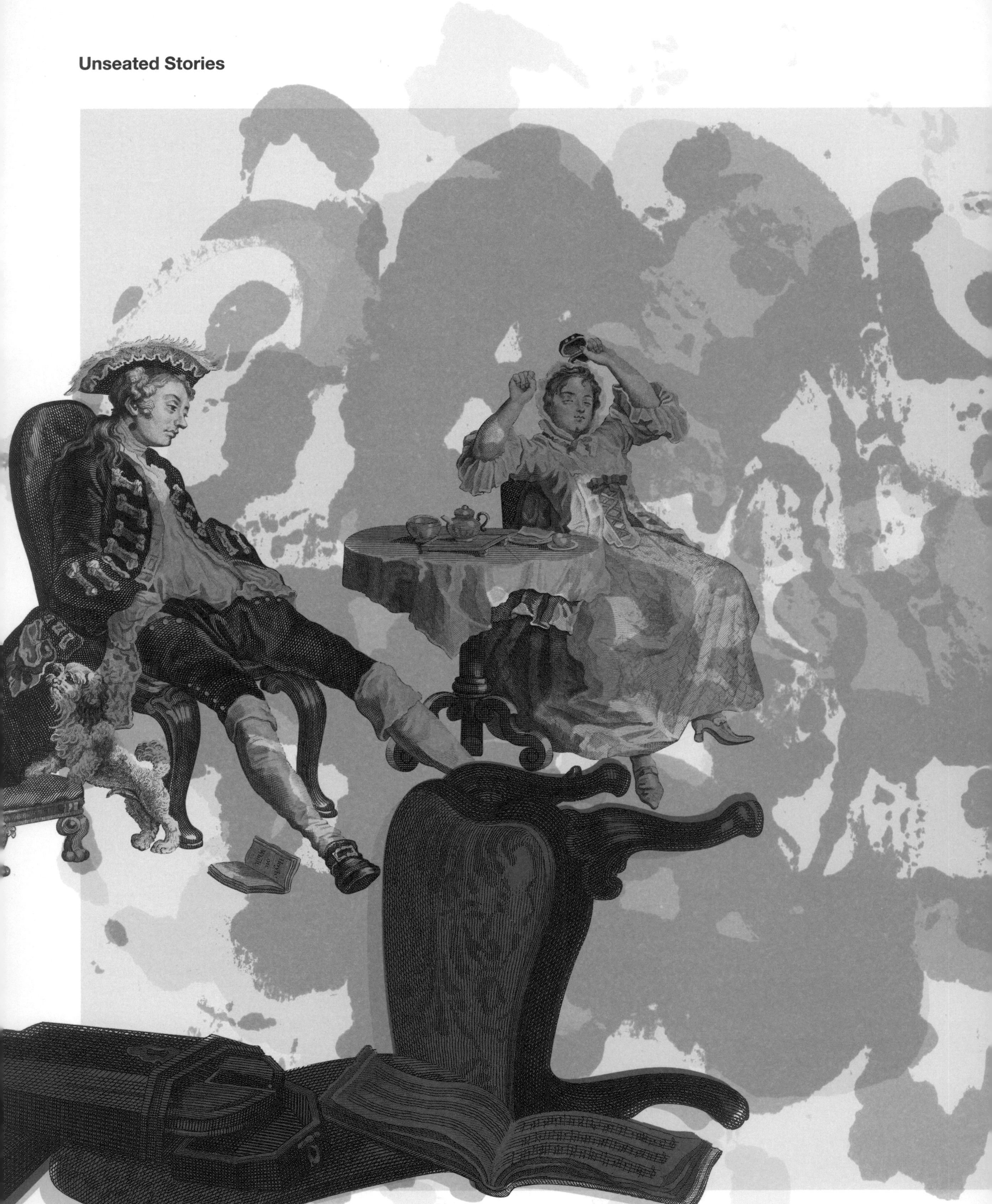

Toppling Chairs, Crumbling Worlds

By Oriol Pibernat

If a chair is lying on the floor, you know something's wrong. The scene depicted by Hogarth confirms it. We see a cluttered, lavishly appointed room. The couple has been married for some time, and if there was ever desire between them, it's gone now—and so is their composure. The lady stretches in a very unladylike gesture. The gentleman is sprawled in his chair, apparently recovering from a night of debauchery. The steward turns away with a horrified expression on his face. The papers in his hands are probably unpaid bills. In the background, another servant raises a hand to his head.

Yet this entire scene of indecency, moral decrepitude, and foreseeable financial ruin can be summed up in an overturned chair. It's a very demure upholstered Queen Anne chair with cabriole legs, but the most important detail is its position on the floor. We're looking at the second of the six prints in the series titled *Marriage À-la-Mode*, engraved by William Hogarth in 1745, * and this isn't the only toppled seat. The fifth print shows a rustic stool kicked over during a skirmish in a bedchamber of secret dalliances. In the sixth and final scene of the drama, another overturned chair occupies the foreground. The household economy has taken a turn for the worse, as denoted by the sight of a humbler apartment and, on the floor, a plebeian, outmoded Renaissance-style chair.

This series tells the story of an arranged marriage between a viscount and a wealthy burgher's daughter, and the inevitable downward spiral into adultery, dissipation, venereal disease, bankruptcy, murder, the gallows, and, finally, suicide. It is a moralizing tale, as well as an illustration of the crumbling of the old social structure, the precepts and rules of hereditary privilege that propped up the *Ancien Régime*. And it can all be summed up in the image of a toppled chair.

* The print series is based on the paintings that Hogarth, with equal narrative skill, had made in 1742.

Proust's Piles of Chairs

By Daniel Cid

Proust's apartment on boulevard Haussmann was crammed with furniture from his family home. After the death of his mother, he felt that house was too steeped in nostalgia and decided to leave, though paradoxically he took as many tables and chairs as he could to his new residence. The extraordinary memoirs of Céleste Albaret, published when she was more than eighty years old, have allowed us to recreate this apartment down to the last detail, as well as the habits of its occupant. All sorts of odds and ends piled up in the unused dining room: mediocre, bourgeois furniture that nevertheless filled the house with memories. Those household items once cherished by his departed loved ones made their absence visible. In any event, none of those chairs were used in the writing process.

Proust liked to work propped up on his bed: white sheets and blank pages. The antithesis of this bed surrounded by Mama's furniture, his writing laboratory, might be the sofa he gave to Le Cuziat, a brothel near his house. The story is repeated in Proust's fictional work *In the Shadow of Young Girls in Flower*, where the Narrator gives a sofa inherited from Aunt Léonie to a whorehouse—the same seat on which he had, as young man, "tasted for the first time the pleasures of love with one of my girl cousins."

Pessoa's Chair

By Daniel Cid

There aren't any photographs of Fernando Pessoa's chair. The ones he had were always rented, and, in any case, he preferred to write standing up, on a tall chest of drawers. And here we have him, in a dingy room in Lisbon that costs him four *reales*, a faded, nondescript fourth-floor apartment where he lives interrogating life, looking at the half-filled page while a cheap cigarette burns down on a piece of blotting paper transformed into a makeshift ashtray. It has just stopped raining; standing, he watches the sunset rays filter through his window. The sky slowly clears, the last drops of accumulated water drain away, and the voices of the city resume their chatter after the rain. He wishes that life was an eternal moment at the window of his rented room, in the intimate plausibility of the fading afternoon. An old coat for morning vigils hangs from a faceless chair, and worn slippers rest on the floor.

Unlike Proust, who built a warm nest lined with decorative objects from his family home, Pessoa only has rented furniture and a trunk as his sole possession. A melancholy denizen of the world, plural like the universe, the only thing he owns is a wooden chest which, by the end of his life, would contain a total of 27,543 semi-orderly handwritten or typed documents. Unpublished texts written on pages, pamphlets, or advertisements. Pessoa reduced the house to a simple rented room shaken by a faith impervious to the truth of the intimate, the ethical and moral foundation of a bourgeois society which lived in purchased homes cluttered with decorative junk.

The Man Who Didn't Know How to Sit

By Santi Barjau

In Barcelona, the year 1931 marked the passing of a tremendously prolific architect with nearly five hundred projects to his name, many of them residential. Over a career spanning nearly half a century, the Marquis of Sagnier had built much of the modern city and even left evidence of his skill in other corners of the world. An obituary extolled the comfort of the homes that Enrique Sagnier Villavecchia had designed and constructed, linking this quality to his own character as a home-loving father and affable man with an active social life: according to the notice, a man like that, who knew how to savor the warmth of hearth and home, was eminently suited to design pleasant houses.

The author of the obituary, fellow architect Pere Benavent, contrasted his case with that of other architects who led more solitary, reclusive lives (perhaps he had Gaudí in mind?). Benavent compared this to the case of a young cabinetmaker he knew, "very competent in the fine skills of his trade," but unsatisfactory when asked to make a chair, as he "didn't know how to sit." By this he meant that the man was not acquainted with the pleasure of sitting comfortably. According to his theory, a man can't create something good unless he's able to enjoy his own creation.

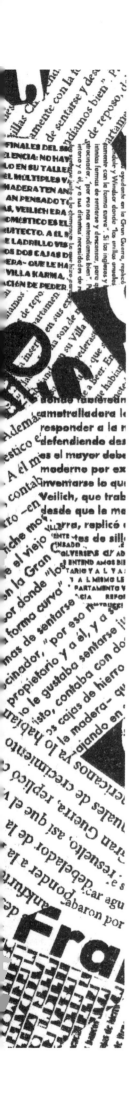

Loos Sits on His Secrets

By José María Faerna

According to Loos, his clients—never many, but a select few—would sometimes ask him, "What will you do when old Veillich is gone?" Josef Veillich made all the chairs for Adolf Loos's houses, from his first projects until the cabinetmaker's death in 1929. The architect published a heartfelt eulogy in the *Frankfurter Zeitung* where, in short, precise machine-gun bursts, he rattled off the ideas about how to satisfy the human need to sit that he had been defending since the end of the previous century. Loos was the great vanquisher of originality, that quintessential modern fetish: there was no need to invent something if the solution already existed, so old Veillich, who had labored alone in his workshop ever since his assistant was killed in the Great War, supplied Loos with skillfully made replicas, multiple variations on Chippendale and Windsor chairs in which "the annual rings of the wood had to line up exactly with the curves." If British and American designers had already thought of everything, all the different ways of sitting and resting, why rack your brain to find something new? Plus, Veillich was deaf like his patron, "so we got on well." For Loos, a domestic interior was the reflection of its owner; therefore he, and his unique needs of rest and repose, should always be the architect's point of reference.

Loos himself liked to sit by the fireside. The brick-faced fireplace he made for his Viennese apartment had two masonry benches which, around 1904, he remodeled so that two iron cases—made of wood in the replica at the Wien Museum—could be inserted at either end. These had been entrusted to him for safekeeping by Doctor Theodor Beer, for whom Loos was building a house on Lake Geneva called Villa Karma. Charged with child molestation, Beer fled Vienna to avoid arrest, but he was eventually convicted and lost his noble title, his job at the University of Vienna, and his wife, who committed suicide. Loos and his friends Karl Kraus and Peter Altenberg vehemently defended Beer. In 1928, Loos himself faced a controversial accusation of child abuse from several girls who had posed for him and was sentenced to four months in prison. His house was searched, and the compromising contents of Beer's cases came to light during the trial. It was useless to protest he had nothing to do with them. Loos, who always knew that designing was essentially about making choices, never actually designed a chair; he confined himself to astutely reforming the ones he had at hand—even the chest of secrets belonging to a friend in a scrape, which ended up becoming his own (the secrets and the scrape). Designs on design. Loos, the first meta-designer.

A Chair for Dr. Freud

By Daniel Cid

Freud liked to read in a rather peculiar position: leaning at a diagonal, legs slung over the arm of the chair, the book held high, and his head unsupported. In order to make this odd posture more comfortable, Freud's daughter Mathilde gave him this chair, designed by the architect Felix Augenfeld in 1930. The numerous Egyptian, Greek, and Asian statuettes that cluttered his desk would have been mute witnesses. Precious because of the histories and stories they represented, these figurines came from the civilizations Freud had studied and interpreted in great detail. They materialized the imaginary assets of psychoanalysis, based on verbal and mental phenomena. These figures offered presence where there was only absence, as repositories of the dreams and myths that allowed psychoanalysis to delve into the earliest stage of human existence.

Looking at a photograph that Engelman took of this chair in 1938, we get the impression that it has just been vacated. Of course, the desk is filled with statuettes, though the eye is drawn particularly to the tall figure of Neith. In predynastic Egypt, Neith was considered an androgynous deity, a transformative quality that Freud found fascinating. The statue was a gift from the Wolf Man. Further to the left, in front of the folder, we see the partly hidden figure of Amun-Re with his distinctive and prominent headdress. Perched on the side table is the Chinese sage with whom Freud always exchanged greetings before sitting down to work. This wise man is accompanied by Imhotep, the physician and architect. All these things were captured in a photograph where the occupant is absent, but traces of him linger. In a rather uncanny, unsettling way, the half-turned chair echoes the routine motions of someone who isn't there. Who knows? Perhaps the real reason for Freud's contorted reading position was that he wanted to share his book with those silent coworkers.

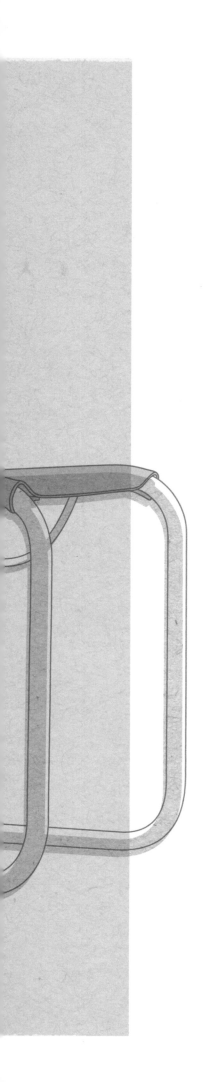

A Conversation on the Train

By Isabel Campi

Everyone agrees that the cantilever chair (called the *Freischwinger* or "free-swinger" in German), based on the principle of the cantilever beam and characterized by its resilience, is a universal design. What people can't agree on is its paternity. Was Marcel Breuer's design inspired by Mart Stam's idea, or vice versa? How did the two designers know each other? At what point did their experiments intersect?

In 1926, the Dutch architect Mart Stam had designed a chair without back legs made of ten straight lengths of gas pipe connected by elbow fittings. As the frame collapsed under the weight of a person, he had to add a brace between the two legs. The chair had no spring at all, but Stam didn't care; his goal was to design a minimal, basic object that would be something like a manifesto of the ideals of modern architecture.

Meanwhile, in 1926 the young Bauhaus professor Marcel Breuer was designing tubular furniture for the Dessau school's new building. One of his concerns was finding steel tubes that were strong yet also resilient enough to produce a two-legged chair with "flex."

Breuer and Stam met on the train from Frankfurt to Stuttgart sometime in 1926 or 1927. Breuer told Stam that he'd begun producing two-legged chairs on a small scale, but he wanted them to be springy and was having a hard time finding the kind of tube. That flexibility was very important to him. Breuer thought he was working for the good of humanity and naively shared his secrets. When he got home, Stam drew Breuer's chair and decided to produce it using tubes with an iron core, which made it robust but not flexible. Later, he began taking protective legal measures.

As a result, in 1929 the companies that manufactured Breuer's and Stam's models became embroiled in a bitter lawsuit over the rights to the *Freischwinger* chair. Anton Lorenz, the businessman who had secured the rights to Stam's design by getting him to sign a contract, defended the originality of the idea, while Thonet—who had recently acquired Standard-Möbel, in which Breuer had a stake—argued that Breuer had made a technical improvement and that his chair was genuinely flexible, an industrial product rather than a workshop experiment. In the end, Lorenz won Breuer's rights and licensed them to Thonet, but he couldn't prevent the proliferation of knockoffs due to the international success of this model, which went on to become a universal archetype.

A Bucket Seat, a Plagiarism Allegation, and the Longest Five Seconds in History

By José María Faerna

The world first learned of the Panton chair in the August 1967 issue of the Danish design journal *Mobilia*, which put it on the cover and meticulously documented it in an exclusive photo essay. But the history of this design began at least eleven years earlier and wouldn't end until 1999 when, one year after Verner Panton's death, Vitra launched its final injection-molded polypropylene version. In fact, Panton claimed that the idea had come to him even earlier, when he was working at Arne Jacobsen's studio and first saw the molded forms of a fiberglass helmet and a plastic bucket: he was particularly struck by how little the bucket cost.

The positive impact of the spread was marred in the following issue of *Mobilia*: a new article by Axel Thygesen questioned the originality of Panton's idea for a one-piece cantilever chair, comparing it to two designs by Gunnar Aagaard Andersen and Poul Kjaerholm from 1953 and 1955, respectively, which were never produced. Thygesen argued that those two projects deserved to be recognized as the forerunners that inspired Panton, but Andersen, a highly regarded professional in the Danish design world at the time, went even further, openly claiming that Panton had stolen his idea. However, *Mobilia* didn't subscribe to the fence-straddling misconception, so common in journalism today, that the truth is the arithmetical average of two lies, and, without attempting to conceal the facts of the dispute from its readers, set the record straight with another article in the same issue by the journal's editor, Svend Erik Møller, defending the August spread. Møller argued that the form of the Panton chair was inseparable from its production method, the result of "an industrial development process in which the designer's work is merely one aspect of a costly, high-risk investment."

There were certainly many similarities between Andersen and Kjaerholm's prototypes, never published or patented, and Panton's formal solution—though he always denied knowledge of both—but they had appeared too soon, when producing them was still a pipe dream given the state of technology. However, Panton chased that dream with steadfast patience and perseverance, undeterred by temporary setbacks or even resounding failures. In 1971, Vitra had begun manufacturing his model in Luran S, a BASF thermoplastic polystyrene that made the chairs cheaper and easier to produce, but in the long run they proved not to be sufficiently weather-resistant, and the company discontinued the line in 1979. And of the original 1967 fiberglass-reinforced polyester version, only around one hundred and fifty units were made.

It was a long road from there to the hundreds of thousands produced of the final version, and only Panton and Vitra walked it together. Jens Bernsen, director of the Danish Design Center in Copenhagen, once told Panton that most of his designs were "jobs basically done in five minutes," to which Verner, shaking his head, replied, "More like five seconds." Bernsen wisely qualified his remark by noting that, in some cases, it takes a lifetime to reach those five seconds—the same lesson Møller and *Mobilia* had tried to teach their readers back in 1967. Back when magazines still existed, and they were still good for something.

Unseated Stories

Mathilde Freud asked the Viennese architect and designer Felix Augenfeld to design a chair for her father. Working with his partner Karl Hofmann, Augenfeld created something truly unique—not just because of its original forms, reminiscent of Henry Moore's sculptures, but also because it was the only one ever made. When Sigmund Freud immigrated to Great Britain in 1938, fleeing from the Nazis, he took it with him. Today it sits in London's Freud Museum. —*Page 195*

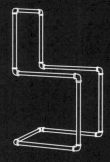

Unauthorized copies or knockoffs are regrettably common in the design business, generating huge losses for those who invest their money and ideas in helping the industry evolve. But coincidences do happen, and two designers—or even three—can come up with the same idea around the same time. Throughout the history of design, there have been all sorts of cases involving alleged plagiarism. Some are quite surprising.

Prototype of the cantilever chair designed by Mart Stam in 1926, made of gas pipe lengths and elbow fittings. Right, the B33 model by Marcel Breuer that Thonet added to its catalogue in 1928–1929. Meanwhile, in 1927 Mies van der Rohe had designed the MR10, manufactured by Berliner Metallgewerbe Josef Müller. Their formal similarities have fueled debates for years. In 2015, the architect Pablo López Martín published a magnificent 400-page doctoral thesis titled "La silla de la discordia" [The Chair of Contention] on the controversy and disputed paternity of the cantilever chair that pitted Breuer, Mies, and Stam against each other in the early days of modernism. —*Page 197*

Verner Panton (1926–1998) became popular for his colorful futuristic creations, so different from traditional Scandinavian design. Yet at the beginning of his career, between 1950 and 1952, he had worked in the studio of another famous Danish artist, Arne Jacobsen, where he helped develop the iconic Ant chair. In 1955 Panton opened his own studio, and in t he early 1960s he knocked on Vitra's door to offer them the chair that bears his name. Its debut in 1967 sparked a controversy. —*Page 199*

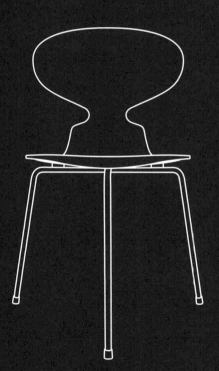

The Ant chair has just three legs and a distinctive ant-like body. The original design from 1952 was replaced three years later by the Series 7. Three-legged chairs aren't often seen on the market, perhaps because we subconsciously perceive them as unsteady, but these don't wobble or topple over.

A book like this wouldn't be complete without Arne Jacobsen (1902–1972). The Danish architect and designer is one of the greatest names in design history: admired, imitated, and copied. The Model 3107 he designed for the firm Fritz Hansen in 1955 is the perfect chair. The seat and back are made of one piece, with a minimalist frame just large enough to support it. It's lightweight, flexible, and stackable. The chair has inspired countless copies, which can be hard to identify at first sight unless you're an expert. But time will tell: knockoffs are always of inferior quality and break easily.

Chairs and Letters

Stevenson, Henry James, Two Chairs, and Five Tables

By José María Faerna

Robert Louis Stevenson always found it hard to sit still. Consumptive and sickly, he lived in many houses, visited many countries, and went to die in Samoa, where the natives, who had no idea that a story could be made up, took all the astonishing tales that Tusitala told them as gospel truth. Perhaps because the doctor had prescribed endless mornings in bed when he was a child, Stevenson had a prickly relationship with chairs; according to his friend, the critic Edmund William Gosse, he always used chairs eccentrically, "with his legs thrown sidewise over the arms of them, or the head of a sofa treated as a perch." Gosse also noted, somewhat enigmatically, that he "very earnestly dealt with us on the immorality of chairs and tables." The restless Louis didn't get along well with furniture designed to promote stillness. In 1885, John Singer Sargent portrayed him in an extraordinary little picture, nervously pacing and talking as he stroked his long, sparse mustache in the drawing room at Skerryvore, the Bournemouth house he had named after one of the lighthouses designed by his grandfather in the Hebrides. It's one of those rare and wonderful portraits that capture the subject so vividly we feel like we're in the room with him.

The previous year, Stevenson had written a description of his ideal home, where the most important room was the studio, very spacious and furnished with two chairs and five tables: one "for actual work, one close by for references in use; one, very large, for MSS. or proofs that wait their turn; one kept clear for an occasion; and the fifth is the map table, groaning under a collection of large-scale maps and charts." A studio where he could flit from table to table and always find plenty of reasons to avoid sitting down. With such a clutter of tables, it's little wonder he only required two chairs, though he did specify that the chair used for writing should be "very low and easy, and backed into a corner." And the wicker chair in which the author of *Treasure Island* posed for Sargent again in 1887 certainly fit that description.

A wicker chair in a dim interior, an outlandish notion in those Victorian times, although Louis has made himself quite comfortable: casually lolling at an angle, taking up the entire surface of the wide seat with his long crossed legs while his consumptive fingers toy with a cigarette. The blue upholstered armchair or settee in which Fanny Stevenson, dressed like an Indian maharani, lounges in the 1885 portrait, barely visible on the far right, is also quite low. In a letter, Stevenson claimed that this chair had belonged to his grandfather, the lighthouse builder, "but since some months goes by the name of Henry James's [chair] for it was there the novelist loved to sit." Too restless to even claim his own furniture, Stevenson named his chairs after another writer.

Edgar Allan Poe's Ghostly Chairs

By José María Faerna

Walter Benjamin called him "the first physiognomist of the domestic interior," because the storytellers of the Early Modern Era provided detailed descriptions of their characters' faces and physical constitutions, but hardly mentioned the rooms they occupied. The first nineteenth-century writer to give interiors a presence in his tales was Edgar Allan Poe, who also wrote two specific works on the subject. One is the short and sarcastic "Philosophy of Furniture," published in May 1840 in *Burton's Gentleman's Magazine* out of Philadelphia, where Poe mocked his fellow countrymen for their poor taste in interior decoration: "It is an evil growing out of our republican institutions, that here a man of large purse has usually a very little soul which he keeps in it." Poe contrasted ostentation with simple elegance and praised the merits of carpets, which should always be thick and feature abstract motifs and arabesques, never plants or naturalistic themes; he despised glare and harsh gas lights, instead favoring the heavy, nuanced, shadowy glow of Argand oil lamps, and held forth on the undesirable "spotty" effect of too many small paintings.

But what did he say about chairs? In his text, Poe described an ideal room glimpsed just before midnight, an oblong chamber with window panes of crimson-tinted glass and silver paper on the walls, providing full details of the picture frames, the Sèvres vases, the effects of the Argand lamp, and the rosewood pianoforte. That space has been reconstructed three times: once for an exhibition at the Brooklyn Museum in 1959; again at the house where the writer lived in Philadelphia, now open to visitors; and the third time only with words, as Poe did, in a short story written by Roberto Bolaño in 1996 called "Edelmira Thompson de Mendiluce," where the heroine, a *fin-de-siècle* Argentine lady, had that room recreated with neurotic exactitude. The two material reconstructions have a rather disappointing Biedermeier feel, and the palpable aura of the Bostonian author's description is conspicuously absent. Both contained two or three Chippendale chairs, which Bolaño also included in his detailed inventory: "Two light conversation chairs, also of rosewood." But Poe's description emphasizes other seats: "Two large low sofas of rosewood and crimson silk, gold-flowered, form the only seats, with the exception of two light conversation chairs, also of rose-wood." Nine years later, just four months before his death, Poe published "Landor's Cottage", a kind of literary tracking shot at sunset that slowly approaches and eventually enters a house in the valley, generally believed to be an idealized version of the cottage Poe inhabited in what was then the countrified New York borough of the Bronx. Here he did include "a few chairs (including a large rocking-chair,) and a sofa, or rather "settee"; its material was plain maple painted a creamy white, slightly interstriped with green—the seat of cane. The chairs and table were "to match"."

Sussex or Windsor-type chairs painted white. Neither the symbolist Edelmira nor the brainy museum curators understood that, in the poet's plush domestic daydreams, chairs are the ghostly presence.

Silleria plegada sistema Aspiazu

Silla

Escala de 0.1 por metro para todas las fig.

2 metros

Sillón

PRIVILEGIO
DE
YNVENCION

Sofá

El Secretario:

Gregorio Aspiazu

Vitoria 15 de Julio de 1872

A Privileged Chair

By Patricio Sáiz

It's certainly a privilege to be allowed to sit on a privileged chair. And I had that privilege in the winter of 2014, on the way to Molledo Portolín, under the long shadow of a cypress tree at the house from which Miguel Delibes once sallied forth to harry his friends the trout.

Between 1826 and 1878, the Spanish system for the protection of industrial property rights relied on "privileges of invention," as patents were peculiarly known here in the nineteenth century. On July 15, 1872, in the middle of the Third Carlist War, a forty-three-year-old master cabinetmaker from Vitoria named Gregorio Azpiazu y Barrutia applied for and was granted one of those privileges, a five-year patent on a new method of constructing folding chairs.

Although no one knows exactly when the first folding chair appeared (probably many centuries ago), the Azpiazu system invented in 1872 had the advantage of "limited fittings or joints," as set out in the patent specifications. Made of wood, the chairs built using this system were less likely to break, "took up less space," and were "highly portable."

Their resilience and longevity are corroborated by the fact that, nearly one hundred and fifty years later, I was able to unfold one of those chairs made in Vitoria and converse while resting in it, as if the intervening years had been folded to the size of that seat. Upholstered, in wicker, rattan, or pierced sheet metal... hundreds, perhaps even thousands of those chairs, in their different versions, have scattered across the length and breadth of Spain.

How one of them ended up in the house on the River Besaya frequented by the writer Miguel Delibes, the setting of his novel *The Path*, will remain one of life's little mysteries best left unsolved. However, having studied thousands of "privileges of invention," when I came across that tangible object in the shadows of Iguña Valley, near Mt. Jano, I remembered the hero of that novel, Daniel "the Owl," and was overcome by the same sentiment as his friend: "The enormous mountains with their ragged peaks, outlined on the horizon, gave Roque an irritating feeling of his own insignificance."

Neruda's Mediterranean Chair

By Mónica Piera

The rush seat is one of the greatest hits in chair history. Invented sometime in the 1600s, demand increased exponentially in the late eighteenth century and has continued to grow ever since. Rush chairs are now hugely popular in Catalonia and the rest of the Mediterranean world.

The secret of its success is the simple, long-lasting construction and, above all, the use of local materials suited to this warm, humid climate with a versatile range of finishes. There have been rush chairs for rich and poor sitters, high and low chairs, wide and narrow, with and without arms, individual seats and settees, stools, benches, reclining and even birthing seats. But one model didn't appear—at least not that we know of—until the twentieth century: the six-legged chair, which lets you lean back without raising the front legs off the ground, with the consequent loss of stability. The idea is so clever and necessary that it must have existed before *Noucentisme*, but so far historians haven't been able to prove it.

The six-legged chair is a reclining seat designed for those sweltering summer afternoons when you just want to lean back and gaze at the horizon. Rodríguez Arias probably discovered it on the open porch of some Catalan farmhouse and decided to call it the Catalana: a stationary version of the rocking chair. The impressive ocean views from Isla Negra in Valparaíso, Chile, where Pablo Neruda chose to make his residence, demanded this relaxing six-legged chair. The GATCPAC architect made his even more comfortable than the ones crafted in Catalonia. In 1942 he added armrests, making them wider and rounded at the ends in keeping with Chilean tradition, and selected materials that were readily available in the South American country to respect the principle of local design. The superb result demonstrates Rodríguez Arias's talent for rethinking traditional furniture to create truly timeless pieces.

Hergé and Prouvé

By Oriol Pibernat

Here's an interesting question: how did an armchair designed by Jean Prouvé end up at a hotel for vacationers in Vargèse? For those who may not know, Vargèse is a small mountain village in the Haute-Savoie invented by Hergé that appeared in the first pages of *Tintin in Tibet*, a comic published in *Tintin* magazine in 1958 and as a book in 1960. * The thrilling adventure that will lead the heroes to the cave of the Yeti himself begins with Tintin, Snowy, Captain Haddock, and Professor Calculus on a pleasant holiday in the Alps. We can image ourselves taking a seat in a corner of the Hôtel des Sommets and settling in for one of those lazy afternoons when time lingers amid plumes of cigar smoke and the aroma *of café au lait*, board games, puzzles, reading, and trivial postcard notes... Suddenly, the calm is shattered by Tintin's loud cry as he awakes from his visionary dream, scaring everyone around him.

Well, in that short comic-strip sequence, we can count as many as seven specimens of the aforementioned armchair. Neither Professor Calculus, absorbed in his reading and deaf to the uproar, nor the rest of the guests probably know that this chair was designed by Jean Prouvé and dates from 1942–1944, although it was not sold until the 1950s. It's also unlikely that they knew the chair was called Visiteur and catalogued as FV 12, or that it preceded a similar but more famous model, the FV 22, known as Kangourou. ** Those prototypes were developed in the golden age of the Maxéville Design Office (1947–1953), where Prouvé launched a revolution in domestic furniture. Hergé must have seen one of those chairs in person or in a photograph featured in some catalogue or magazine. Curious and with a keen eye for detail, Hergé and his assistants were always on the lookout for new items to furnish his hypnotizing comics. His passion for research is legendary. And this scene gave him a chance to show off his drawing skills. It's tempting to imagine a kind of spiritual connection, that the spirit of the industrial artisan in Hergé the comic-book artist somehow reached out to the soul of the studio engineer in Prouvé. One took the light way and the other the solid. One sketched and the other built. But something generational in their genius and something personal in their aesthetic language led them to furnish that page together.

* We Tintinologists never miss a chance to show off our knowledge of such stupid trivia.

** More obscure facts we scholars of design like to collect (design enthusiasts can be just as annoying as Tintinologists). And here's a theory about the chair's name: the second model of the armchair, FV 22, replaced the metallic back legs with wooden side braces that extended beyond the chair back. This made the seat look rather like a kangaroo, resting on powerful wooden haunches with little metal forelegs sticking out at the front. The soft cushions in the lap of this marsupial seat were perfect for cradling both flesh-and-blood sitters and fictional characters.

Chairs and Letters

Sussex Chairs were made by Morris & Company, a decorating firm founded by William Morris in 1861 in Victorian England. The company worked with architects and artists like the painter Ford Madox Brown (1821–1893), who is credited with inventing the Sussex chair.

Windsor Chairs take their name from the English town where the craftsman who began making them in the early eighteenth century had his workshop. Derived from garden furniture, the Windsor chair has a back of thin spindles set into a solid wooden seat. —*Page 205*

Germán Rodríguez Arias (1902–1987), born in Barcelona, was one of the architects responsible for bringing rationalism to Catalonia. He founded the GATCPAC [Group of Catalan Architects and Experts for the Advancement of Contemporary Architecture] along with Sert, Torres Clavé, and others. After the Spanish Civil War, he became an exile in Chile, where he continued working as an architect and designer. He also founded a company, Muebles Sur, that made Mediterranean-inspired furniture. He designed the Café Miraflores in the capital, and there he met the poet Pablo Neruda, who gave him several commissions, including the enlargement of Neruda's home in Isla Negra. In 1942 he designed the Catalana chair for that house. Today the model is produced by Mobles 114. —*Page 209*

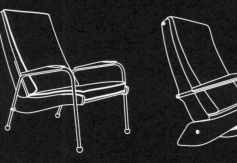
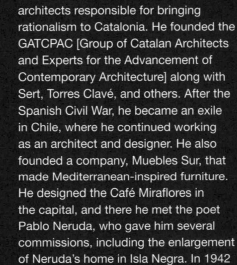

The Visiteur armchair or FV 12 that appears in the adventures of Tintin, and its successor, the FV 22 or Kangourou. Jean Prouvé (1901–1984) was born in the French town of Nancy and was apprenticed to a blacksmith in his youth, where he learned metalworking techniques. In 1924 he founded Ateliers Jean Prouvé, where he developed numerous furniture designs with industrial materials and systems for modular prefabricated structures. One of the prototypes was assembled to serve as his office in Maxéville, another town in the Nancy district, where he had opened his own factory in 1947. —*Page 211*

Hergé and other cartoonists like Joost Swarte have furnished their comics with pieces from the real world. The Dutch artist even dedicated some of his stories to the chairs designed by his compatriot Gerrit Rietveld. But it's rare for an India ink chair to materialize in the pages of a manufacturer's catalogue.

In 1987 Mariscal designed the Garriri chair with the same strokes as his lifelong companions and comic-book characters, the Garriris. Produced by the Basque company Akaba, the chair was created for *Nouvelles tendances*, an exhibition organized by the Centre Pompidou in Paris to mark its tenth anniversary. It became an icon of Spanish design in the 1980s.

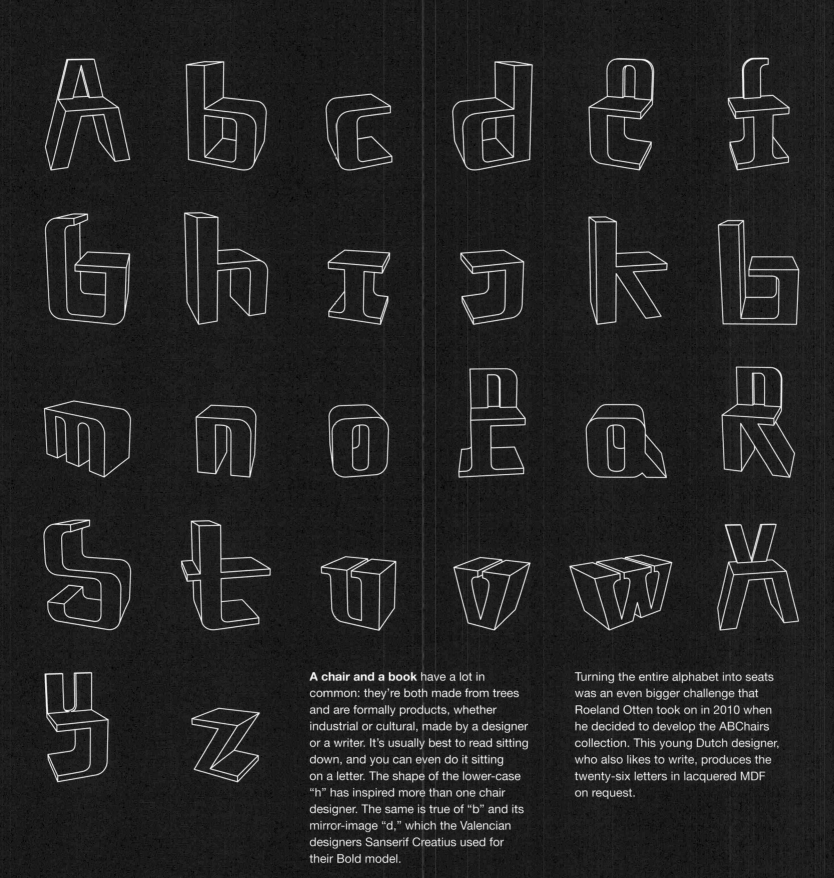

A chair and a book have a lot in common: they're both made from trees and are formally products, whether industrial or cultural, made by a designer or a writer. It's usually best to read sitting down, and you can even do it sitting on a letter. The shape of the lower-case "h" has inspired more than one chair designer. The same is true of "b" and its mirror-image "d," which the Valencian designers Sanserif Creatius used for their Bold model.

Turning the entire alphabet into seats was an even bigger challenge that Roeland Otten took on in 2010 when he decided to develop the ABChairs collection. This young Dutch designer, who also likes to write, produces the twenty-six letters in lacquered MDF on request.

Sillez.

1. La esencia de lo que significa ser una silla.
2. Las cualidades que hacen que una silla sea lo que es.
3. Vivir permanentemente entre sillas.
4. Común en el imaginario colectivo en cuanto a la percepción de lo sustancial de las sillas (según *Alberto Lievore*).

Cuando se habla de la Historia del Arte, en realidad se habla de la historia de los estilos, es decir, las diversas formas a través de las cuales, los hombres sensibles trataban de expresar *Aquello*, lo intangible pero sensible de su experiencia de vida.

El Arte ha gozado siempre de una total libertad de maneras para explorar los pliegues del infinito misterio de la vida y, a pesar de haberlo representado, de miles de modos diversos a través de los tiempos, *Aquello* sigue, silencioso, invisible, sugiriendo que alguien intente explicarlo, mostrarlo, una vez más.

En el modesto oficio de diseñar, esa libertad para representar no solo tiene una escala muy pequeña, está cautiva de la función, es tener que bailar bien, pero con los pies atados. No obstante, esta necesidad de representar valores o de reconocernos en ellos, insiste en nosotros, realizarnos en símbolos, representar, es nuestra condición.

¿Pero cómo se puede pensar otra silla más?, ¿la es, porque nunca se llega con ella a decirlo todo. Todo, como el horizonte, es un sitio a donde llevó a realizar ese modelo?, ¿cuál ha sido el proceso de lo superficial, lo aparente, lo que hace a lo último probablemente, lo aparente. La realidad es que las anteriores diseñadas por nosotros, y en toda y esta a su vez, en todas las anteriores sillas vistas y en las vistas sin saberlo. Aquello que tiene en común todas ellas, aquello que atraviesa tus siempre aquello que las hace próximas, nuestras, aquello que es la esencia de todas las sillas: la sillez... o simplemente Aquello.

30 aniversario de la BDI, Andreu World.

Alberto Lievore's Chairness

By Ramón Úbeda

Chairness* is a concept I learned from Alberto Lievore when Andreu World asked me to put together a book to celebrate the company's fiftieth anniversary. I immediately thought it would make a great title for that history. In the end, however, we went with the more explicit *Chairs*, so I decided to save the idea for another time—and now that time has come. I can't think of a better title for this final chapter of the *Chairpedia*. We could keep adding to it, for there's no shortage of chair stories, but there aren't that many people who live or have lived in a permanent state of *chairness*—another possible use or meaning for the word.

When the Argentine designer first began to collaborate with Andreu World, its founder was still very much present: Francisco Andreu had inherited his father's cabinetmaking workshop at age seventeen and turned it into a world-renowned furniture company. When commissioning a new chair, Andreu always knew exactly what he wanted from the designer: something unique, worth the investment, and, if possible, not too costly to produce. Alberto met all three conditions when he designed the Radical chair in the early 1990s, shortly after forming the Lievore Altherr Molina partnership. They chose that name because it's the ultimate refinement of the universal chair concept, the synthesis of all chairs, a constructive and formal manifesto. It wasn't the first chair the partners made for the Valencian manufacturer, and it certainly wouldn't be the last.

In the foreword to that book, Lievore asked, "But how can there always be one more chair to invent?" before going on to answer his own question: "Perhaps because there's always something left unsaid. Like the horizon, everything is an unattainable idea." If you ask him how he came to create that model, he would say that, in reality, the process began with all the chairs he had designed before, right back to the very first, which in turn may have been influenced by all the chairs he saw in the past. It began with what they all have in common, what endures through the ages, what the essence of all chairs is to him.

* Chairness
1. The essence of what it means to be a chair.
2. The qualities that make a chair what it is.
3. Living permanently among chairs.
4. Common perception of the essence of chairs in the collective imaginary (according to Alberto Lievore).

A Chair Named Desire

By Carmen Sevilla

When the Miss Blanche chair was in production, Shiro Kuramata reportedly phoned the workers at the factory every thirty minutes to make sure the roses floated in the acrylic of the back and arms. Designers, like artists, are often obsessively compulsive about their work. Everything has to be just as they've imagined it, just like the sketches that attempt to capture the reality of their fantasy. They also say that Kuramata traveled all over Japan searching for the kind of artificial roses that would perfectly represent the frailty and vanity of the character Blanche DuBois in the film *A Streetcar Named Desire.*

Prissy, refined, elegant, affected. The Miss Blanche is as pretentious as the character that inspired it; it aspires to be what it isn't. Forever young, like the vain, artificial paper flowers, unbreathing and scentless. Fragile and pretty, hoping to be treated like a delicate lady. It wants to be admired rather than used, observed in the plastic beauty it believes will never fade. If we use it, the chair will soon wither and fade; the acrylic will become scratched and the cloudiness of time will hide the deceptive freshness of its blooms from sight. Kuramata knew that these flowers had to be as false as the farce kept up by Blanche DuBois that ultimately drove her mad.

The chair plays with our perception of space, blending into it, disintegrating before our very eyes. The acrylic tricks us with its transparency, trying to fade into the background yet simultaneously stand out against it.

Sometimes life is so hard that fiction is the only way to survive. As a child, Shiro Kuramata's nickname was *usotsuki* or "fibster," perhaps because he, like Tennessee Williams's character, had a habit of making up stories to conceal his weaknesses.

Falsehood and frailty can be moving. We can look at this chair, but we shouldn't sit on it.

50 Manga Chairs

By Ana Domínguez

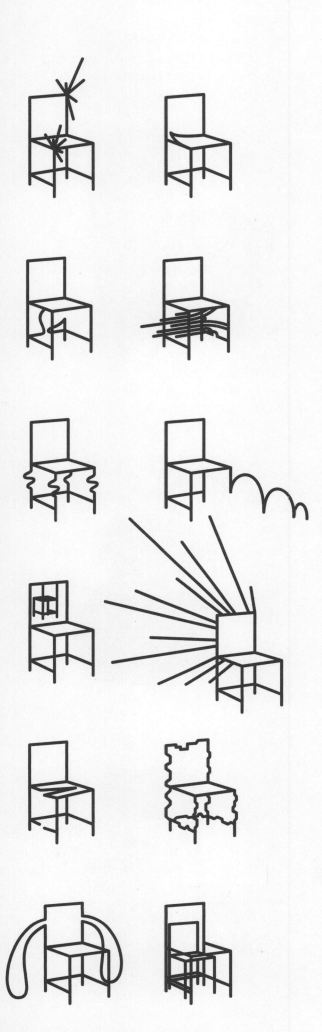

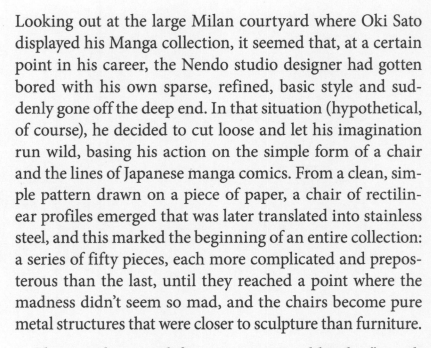

Looking out at the large Milan courtyard where Oki Sato displayed his Manga collection, it seemed that, at a certain point in his career, the Nendo studio designer had gotten bored with his own sparse, refined, basic style and suddenly gone off the deep end. In that situation (hypothetical, of course), he decided to cut loose and let his imagination run wild, basing his action on the simple form of a chair and the lines of Japanese manga comics. From a clean, simple pattern drawn on a piece of paper, a chair of rectilinear profiles emerged that was later translated into stainless steel, and this marked the beginning of an entire collection: a series of fifty pieces, each more complicated and preposterous than the last, until they reached a point where the madness didn't seem so mad, and the chairs become pure metal structures that were closer to sculpture than furniture.

Elements borrowed from manga art—like the "speech bubble" indicating that someone is about to speak, or the "effect lines" that emphasize an action or speed, as well as emotional symbols such as sweat or tears—were added to the original chair to enhance its expressiveness, making it seem as if the entire group is trying to tell us a story. The transition from paper to metal was absolutely literal, and the chairs look like they were drawn in the air, an impression reinforced by the fact that they are entirely devoid of color and texture, which deliberately underscores the abstract nature of manga. Yet the mirrored finish of the chairs causes them to reflect the world around them, so that their "skin" varies depending on where they are placed. Diversity, yes, but within a certain order.

100 Chairs in 100 Days

By Ana Domínguez

Martino Gamper has the soul of an artisan/thinker. He's always liked working with his hands, but exploring his own creativity is one of his guiding principles. In 2007, that combination inspired him to take on a project called "100 Chairs in 100 Days", in which he made a new chair every day for one hundred days from pieces found on the street or in friends' homes (some, like Ron Arad, even donated seats to the project). But this creativity had certain restrictions (after all, Gamper is a designer, not an artist): he could only use the materials available to him on that particular day. No cheating allowed. Sometimes he combined totally dissimilar pieces, other times he found elements that had the same style or production method, and in some cases he patched bits and pieces together in an unthinkable and seemingly irrational way.

The result might be a grotesque hybrid, a poetic assemblage, or even a humorous hodgepodge. But, most importantly, it was an exercise that questioned how we perceive objects when they're removed from their normal context. We don't judge an office chair the same way we do a lawn chair, and we see them differently if we know who designed them. Combining parts of different chairs in one, often in an irreverent way with no regard for categories, raises a lot of questions. Those categories come under scrutiny: certain details that denote luxury may be degraded by association with a lowly element, but the same combination can ennoble a piece of plebeian origins. Who knows? The subject is open to debate. Ultimately, as Gamper himself admits, perfect design doesn't exist, and objects speak to us in a personal way, so the affection we develop for things is different in each individual.

How To Make a Chair

By Daniel Giralt-Miracle

Examine different kinds of wood and choose the one whose grain pattern and color you like best:

Beech – Birch – Black poplar – Boxwood – Cedar
Cherry – Chestnut – Ebony – Elm – Holm oak – Mahogany
Maple – Oak – Olive – Pine – Teak – Walnut – etc.

Remember, the basic parts of a chair are:

Back post – Front legs – Rail – Rear legs – Seat
Splat – Stretcher

However, you can add whatever decorative flourishes and features you find most pleasing:

Acanthus leaf – Apron – Arms – Cockleshell
Ears – Palmette – Patera – Rinceau – Shoe – Volutes – etc.

Assemble the tools you think you'll need:

Adze – Bow lathe – Brace – Carving chisel
Firmer chisel – Glue Gouge – Hammer – Handsaw
Mortise chisel – Rabbet plane – Sander – Screwdriver
Screws – Smoothing plane – etc.

Find a model from the past or present that you like, or be original and invent your own, and get to work. If you come up with a new type of seat, you'll go down in history. But don't forget that a chair isn't a sculpture; it's a form with a specific function.

Chairness

The Story of Andreu World

By Ramón Úbeda

The chair is the undisputed monarch of the furniture world. Chairs tell the entire history of design, for few great designers have been able to resist their allure. Some, like Thonet, Jacobsen, and the Eameses, spent their entire lives in a state of permanent chairness, leaving us an unforgettable legacy and memory. Today there are also designers and companies whose sole purpose in life is to keep on inventing and producing contraptions for sitting. The one thing they all have in common, a quality that endures through the ages and defines the essence of all chairs, is *chairness*, which was going to be the title of a book that ended up being published as *Chairs. 50 años de diseño y una historia que contar* [Chairs: 50 Years of Design and a Story to Tell]. That story is the history of Andreu World.

In the foreword to that book, Jorge Wagensberg wrote, "Chair and buttock are two closely related concepts, but there can be no doubt that the buttock came first." Our buttocks are a product of natural selection. They appeared when the first primates came down from the treetops and began to walk the earth as *Homo erectus*, who kicked off the bipedal craze and invented fire to boot. A million years have passed since then. We know the human species has evolved quite a bit, but there are still many people who prefer to take a load off the old-fashioned way, kneeling or squatting with their backsides resting on their calves. In Western culture, that padded part of our anatomy is also essential when sitting on surfaces that are often hard, in part because we human beings—some more than others—are sedentary creatures and spend something like a hundred thousand hours of our lives in that position, engaging in all sorts of activities. We sit down to eat, work, rest, and entertain ourselves—for instance, at the movies or in a football stadium.

They say even the ancient Egyptians had various types of chairs for sitting in different positions. But those seats must have been reserved for a privileged few because we always see the scribes working on the floor, and because the chair didn't really become available to all social classes until well into the Renaissance. The birth of the Savonarola chair in late fifteenth-century Italy marked the beginning of the democratic history of this piece of furniture, which went on to become the most frequently designed object of the Modern Era. As stated above, we can trace this history through the work of the most important architects and designers, with every confidence that none will be overlooked, and tell the story of the chair in connection with the development of materials and industry, aesthetic and typological revolutions and evolutions, and the technical and ergonomic discoveries that enhanced its performance. We've also evolved in this area, and today we can find chairs tailored to every kind of preference and activity. There are thousands upon thousands of models, and new ones appear every day. We can even find examples of chairs in which functionality is not an essential requirement.

From Workshop to Factory

"A chair can even be used for sitting, but only on the condition that one sits uncomfortably." Salvador Dalí said this when he drew the Leda chair in his painting *Femme à la tête rose* (1935). Spain's universal artist, who was also a designer and friend of the well-known furniture maker Jean-Michel Frank, obviously never met Francisco Andreu, who undoubtedly would have enlightened him on the myriad benefits of a comfortable seat. Andreu's way of thinking was only natural for someone born far from Paris's elitist artistic circles, a man who had learned his trade in a cabinetmaker's workshop and begun making his first chairs when he was barely seventeen years old, at a time—the 1950s—when Spain was still struggling to overcome chronic shortages and hardships. Working without electricity at his family's residence in the town of Alaquàs, on the outskirts of Valencia, young Andreu began making chairs that initially imitated the classic, popular, anonymous models of that period. The first, produced in 1955, was known simply as Model 1.

The young cabinetmaker began selling his homemade creations in furniture stores and via traveling salesmen, using carts to deliver his chairs and waiting for a chance to turn his craft into a business. That chance came with the arrival of electricity. He equipped a 345-square-foot workshop with a power saw, sander, drill, and other tools that enabled him to work in better conditions and add more stylized designs to his product catalogue, like the Model 72 chair from 1957. The business seemed to be doing well, so at age twenty-three Francisco Andreu opened a new 2100-square-foot building, also at the back of his family home. Later came the first trips abroad, which inspired Scandinavian-style chairs such as the Model 123 in 1963. For Andreu, as for other Spanish entrepreneurs of that period, visits to international fairs were an eye-opening experience, and he became eager to manufacture avant-garde chairs that would still serve their primary purpose as seating devices.

Soon he was ready to take the next big step—though fate practically made it inevitable, as the company had to move after an accident destroyed the production facility. The new location, with 8600 square feet, was a proper factory, and it opened with a proper name: Curvados Andreu. A medium-sized enterprise with forty employees, growing slowly but steadily. As production increased, it gradually absorbed other nearby workshops and built up a countrywide sales network. It wasn't easy; as the sales representatives didn't have catalogues, they had to cart the chairs across the country in their cars so potential customers could see the merchandise. However, the system did have one advantage: it ensured close quality control throughout the entire process, from manufacturing (and upholstering) to final sale. All the company needed now was a steady supply of raw material: better wood, and more of it. Francisco Andreu traveled to Singapore, Malaysia, Indonesia, and even Brazil to make sure that neither foreign oak nor exotic mahogany could compete with the beech wood they'd been using up to that point, which could be found right here in Spain, in the neighboring region of Navarre.

The Story of Andreu World

Near a beech forest, the company established a sawmill and later a new factory called Andreu Nort. The old Alaquàs factory continued to operate under a new name, Andreu Est.

Down the path of design

In the 1970s, the company ran like clockwork. It had secured a reliable source of raw material, improved production, and reinforced logistics thanks to the purchase of new storage and dispatch machinery. But the only way to keep growing and enter new markets was to head down the path of design. Their first steps were cautious: they launched a new product line that incorporated external creativity, but at the same time they maintained the one that had worked well so far, just in case. The new catalogues were called Iberchair and Slae Design. They had English names and international ambitions, but their DNA was still one hundred percent Valencian. The first designers Andreu hired were local talents. Ximo Roca, Vicente Soto, Ángel Martí, Ángel Tíscar, and the sorely missed Pedro Miralles preceded the wave of Barcelona-based designers who came on board later, including Nancy Robbins, Quod, Bernal & Isern, Josep Mora, Jorge Pensi, Gabriel Teixidó, and Pete Sans. The plans for international expansion prospered, and when it began exporting products in the 1980s, Curvados Andreu changed its name to Andreu World. Serious graphic design also came into play with a new logo drawn by Mario Eskenazi.

But the grand coming-out party took place in 1998, and the blushing debutante was a chair named Andrea, designed by Josep Lluscà; Francisco Andreu's dream of bringing avant-garde seats to market had finally come true. Lluscà's chair was definitely a cutting-edge design. With its three-legged aluminum frame and carved wooden body, it was a genuine showpiece, a pearl worthy of the glossiest magazines, and confirmation of the company's commitment to offering unique products that would set it apart from the rest. Distinction came at a cost, but Andreu World was up to the challenge: it invested in design, taking risks on new projects and creating the reliable in-house technical department it needed to pursue them, and in communications, with new catalogues, advertising campaigns in industry magazines, and a revamped brand image that would later be entrusted to another Valencian with talent and personality, Antonio Solaz (the gifted illustrator of this *Chairpedia*). All these investments paid off, but the one that really made a difference was undoubtedly the recruitment of a talented trio: Alberto Lievore, Jeanette Altherr, and Manel Molina.

Mies van der Rohe once said, "A chair is a very difficult object. A skyscraper is almost easier." Perhaps he exaggerated a bit, but he wasn't entirely wrong. Designing a good chair is no easy task, and designing more than one good chair is a feat that only a handful of highly specialized professionals can hope to accomplish. Some designers, like Lievore, live in a permanent state of chairness (he came up with the idea) and are capable of turning out one chair after another without lowering their enviably high standards. Alberto Lievore arrived at Andreu World with the Lynn chair in 1989, when the firm was still basking in the afterglow of Andrea's success. From that moment on, his work for the company, in collaboration with his partners Altherr and Molina, has been fundamental. Not only has he proved that he designs in an almost perpetual state of grace, producing pivotal pieces that have defined the identity of the Andreu World catalogue in recent years—the Radical chair, the best-selling Manila series, the award-winning Smile, and his outdoor collection, to name a few—but he has also made invaluable contributions in other areas, from discreet art direction to the construction of the brand's impeccable visual identity at trade fairs and even the showroom in the Olimar building just outside Valencia, where the company also has its headquarters.

Material culture and industrial culture

"The chair is that thing comprised of a few legs, a seat, and a back." Alessandro Mendini gave this definition at the beginning of his textual tribute to Vico Magistretti, another master of the art of sitting. In that same text, he said more profound things, such as "The chair is the Cartesian axis of Western man," and "The chair is a Bob Wilson show." The construction of any chair, no matter how simple it may look, is also profound and complex. In fact, the simpler it looks, the harder it is to make. The Radical is a case in point. For starters, you've got to have material culture; you need to know that the best wood for building it is oak, because it's dense and resilient. And then you've got to have industrial culture in order to work with it. Countless tasks—preparatory, processing, and finishing jobs—are involved in shaping each individual piece. On the Radical, later rechristened the RDL, a single side has five separate pieces that require a total of thirty different processes. The adventure of manufacturing a chair begins in the forest and ends in the crate that will ship it to its final destination.

The Olimar building, where the head offices and showroom of Andreu World are located, doesn't smell like sawdust. The machinery and the workers are at the factories in Valencia (Andreu Est and Andreu Tops) and Navarre (Andreu Nord), which produce chairs and tables for private homes and corporate customers. The Olimar team's job is to make sure the furniture can be shipped anywhere in the world, thanks to the firm's tight-knit sales network and international presence. Andreu World, which currently exports 85 percent of its total production, has showrooms across the globe, from Chicago and Dubai to Gurugram, India. This significant global expansion was made possible by hard work, but the decision to add pieces by Santiago Miranda & Perry King, William Sawaya, and Mario Bellini—respected names in the Italian design industry—to the Andreu catalogue also helped. Andreu World made the smart decision to produce Sawaya's Zarina and relaunch the Cartesius table Bellini had designed in 1962, for which he won the first of his eight Compasso d'Oro Awards—a historic achievement, being the first time this distinction was awarded to a piece of furniture made in Italy. Perhaps the Valencian firm didn't make a profit on it, but it certainly brought satisfaction and a cultural cachet that's ultimately reflected in the bottom line.

The Story of Andreu World

The last fifteen years have consolidated Andreu World as one of the leading names in the industry, recognized at home with the National Design Prize in 2007 and applauded around the world for its commitment to sustainability. There aren't many furniture companies that manufacture all their products using only FSC-certified wood from their own responsibly cultivated and replanted forests. That is one of the Andreu World hallmarks. Another is the commitment to innovation in both craft and technology, always striving for technical excellence. This blend of tradition and modernity is something worth preserving. Jesús Llinares, current CEO and director of the company, likes to call it "industrializing craftsmanship." Developing production capacity is essential for growing bigger, but investing in good design is highly recommended for growing better. Recruiting Piergiorgio Cazzaniga was a smart move, and getting Patricia Urquiola, Jasper Morrison, and Alfredo Häberli to sign on gave the team a solid reputation in the profession. They've recently been joined by PearsonLloyd and Layer, the design agency owned by Benjamin Hubert, whose sights are set firmly on the future.

For successful entrepreneurs, giving back part of what society has given them is practically an obligation. Reissuing a historic table, publishing a book like this one, or offering a prize that creates opportunities for young designers—since 2001 Andreu World has regularly organized the International Design Contest, now in its twentieth year—are initiatives that make a difference and explain why such a company deserves to be acknowledged and applauded. Having lived and celebrated sixty-five years of history, Andreu World is now in the prime of its *chairness* and eager to continue the adventure, without forgetting its roots or the defining qualities that have made it a brand of and for the world: its identity as a manufacturer that prides itself on quality woodwork, its strong Valencian character that represents the industry of an entire region, and, finally, its nature as a family business. This is an important point, because there aren't many left. The Andreu family, like the Fluxàs at Camper and the Rieras at Metalarte, also distinguished with the National Design Prize, are a rare breed among global design fauna, and well worth preserving.

This text, originally titled "La sillez" [Chairness], is a slightly updated version of the one I wrote when Andreu World was awarded the National Design Prize in 2007, more than half a century after Francisco (Paco) Andreu founded the company. He passed the torch on to his children, Melchor and María Teresa, who have kept it burning with the help of an extraordinary team led by Jesús Llinares. In 2017, Paco passed away in Valencia at the age of seventy-nine, having created an internationally successful firm and fulfilled his dream of becoming part of the history of chairs. This *Chairpedia* is part of the fruits of his labor.

Chairness

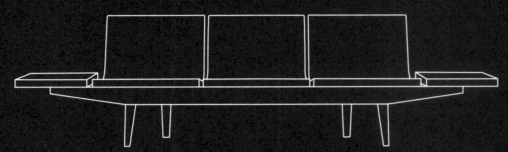

The Radical chair is made entirely of solid oak with a thin curved oak veneer. In 2002 it was renamed the RDL to make its radicalness even more graphic.
—Page 215

Alberto Lievore's collaboration with Andreu World officially began in 1989, when he designed the Lucrecia and Lynn chairs on his own. Soon afterwards, he established a creative partnership with the Lievore Altherr Molina studio, and in 1991 they designed the Radical chair. Since then, their contributions to the company's catalogue have been essential, abundant, and of outstanding quality, with designs like the Trienal bench (1993) and the Manila (1999), Carlotta (2002), Lineal (2003), Ronda (2003), Carola (2004), Brandy (2006), and Smile (2006) chairs.

He also served as art director for a time, a less tangible but equally important job.

Lievore Altherr Molina received the National Design Prize in 1999, the same year they created the Manila chair and its product family, which also includes armchairs, stools, and easy chairs. Like most of their designs, over time the Molina has evolved into a classic.

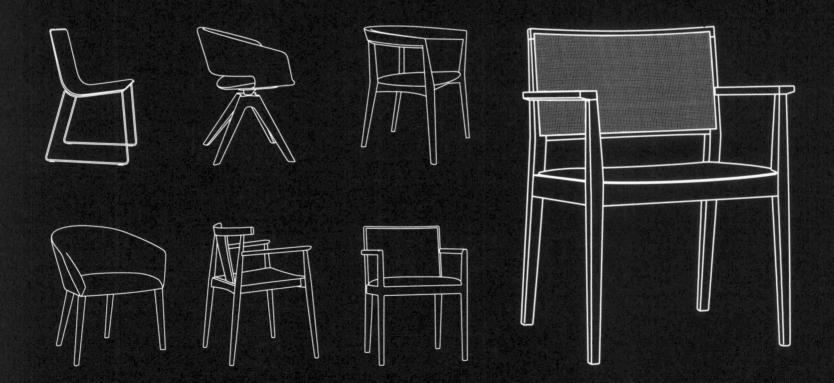

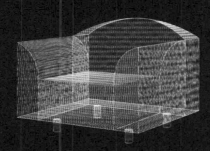

Shiro Kuramata ((1934–1991) designed the Miss Blanche chair for the Ishimaru company in 1988, when the Japanese architect and designer was in his prime. That same year, he decided to move his studio to Paris. Shortly before, he had designed other seats that became famous: the Sing Sing Sing chair for XO (1985) and the easy chair How High the Moon (1986), produced by Vitra.

It was the high point of his professional career. Kuramata's refined, poetic, spiritual, minimalist, ethereal style was put to good use by his fellow countryman Issey Miyake, for whom he designed several stores. He was a master and a singular artist who left us before his time, leaving few works and a gaping hole. —*Page 217*

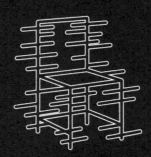

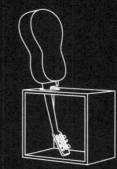

Nendo is a multidisciplinary Japanese design studio directed by Okio Sato, whose creative hyperactivity sets him apart from everyone else. The studio created fifty versions of the chair for this project, but they could have easily made a lot more. Each one has a different personality. And they're all perfect. The chairs were designed in 2016 for the Friedman Benda Gallery in New York and were shown for the first time as an installation at the Basilica Minore di San Simpliciano in Milan, the city where the studio has its European office. —*Page 219*

Nendo's collaboration with Friedman Benda began in 2009 with the show *Ghost Stories*, where the studio exhibited its famous Cabbage chair, created the previous year for the xxist Century Man exhibition curated by Issey Miyake to mark the first anniversary of the Tokyo museum 21_21 Design Sight.

Martino Gamper is a London-based Italian designer. His "100 Chairs in 100 Days" project made him famous around the world. Spending one hundred consecutive days (and nights) thinking up a different chair for each new dawn is a feat worthy of the *Guinness Book of World Records*. The resulting collection, owned by the Milan gallery Nilufar, was exhibited in the British capital in 2007, at the Triennale di Milano in 2009, at the YBCA in San Francisco in 2010, and at the City Gallery Wellington in New Zealand in 2017. All the pieces are depicted and documented in a book by the same name. —*Page 221*

The Chair Is...

By Alessandro Mendini

While the chair works, the man rests.

The chair is that thing comprised of a few legs, a seat, and a back.
The chair is chair, armchair, divan, ottoman, stool, and bench.
The chair is the spatial dimension inside every house.
The chair is made of wood, plastic, marble, fabric, iron, flesh, diamonds, earth.
The chair is the Cartesian axis of Western man.
The chair is sometimes a folding, stackable, swiveling mechanism.
The chair is a swing for banishing thoughts.
The chair is a mode of rest not suitable for animals.
The chair is an object that can take any form.
The chair is a display of virtuosity for any designer.
The chair is synonymous with Thonet.
The chair is the madness of Charles Rennie Mackintosh.
The chair is a bundle of money to buy a Knoll by Saarinen.
The chair is called a "seating system" by experts.
The chair is a place of exclusion for women.
The chair is an office building's stock of thousands of chairs.
The chair is that thing that stalks you every morning.
The chair is the guarantee that you have a job.
The chair is the worker facing the machine.
The chair is a group of frightened children facing the teacher.
The chair is sixteen hours from Rome to Tokyo.
The chair is speeding in a car as the wheels spin underneath.
The chair is a Bob Wilson show.
The chair is a relaxation technique.
The chair is a way of getting men to interact.
The chair is millions of men seated at once.
The chair is a way to have someone sitting opposite in another chair.
The chair is an invention for striking up conversations.
The chair is a pretext for family dinners.

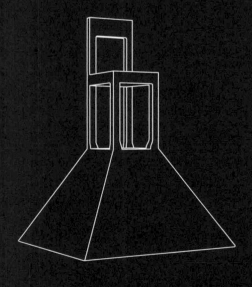

The chair is a circle of people around a guitar on the beach.
The chair is a tatami mat for drinking tea.
The chair is waiting for a delayed flight.
The chair is the tapestry of Buddha and his infinite gaze.
The chair is the throne where monarchs have dozed.
The chair is the bench from which sentences are handed down.
The chair is as big as the whole world placed beneath you.
The chair is a meadow where you can rest when you're short of breath.
The chair is swinging your legs over the Grand Canyon in Colorado.
The chair is the trunk severed at the base.
The chair is the flank of a galloping horse.
The chair is a friendly prosthesis of the human body.
The chair is, to a child, its mother's arm.
The chair is the body of a friend.
The chair is crossing your legs.
The chair is squatting on your own haunches for lack of a chair.
The chair is the instrument of the sedentary.
The chair is the refuge of the weary.
The chair is like a bed that's impossible to sleep on.
The chair is the mirage of the elderly.
The chair is my father in the hospital for the past four years.
The chair is a handkerchief laid on the step to avoid soling the blue dress.
The chair is the stool in the corner of a cell.
The chair is that vague dream in church during a funeral.
The chair is the asphalt where the suicidal protester sets himself on fire.
The chair is the place of electrical death.
The chair is the moment before the garrote snaps your neck.
The chair is sitting on thorns.
The chair is seeing the back of the rickshaw man.
The chair is the sidewalk where the beggar holds out his hand.
The chair will be the void below me if I leap out the window.

A short homage in the form of a poem, read by Mendini in 1980 on the occasion of the *20 anni / 20 sedie* exhibition dedicated to the work of Italian master Vico Magistretti (1920–2006). Both belonged to an inimitable generation of designers who are gradually disappearing.

Alessandro Mendini (1931–2019) left us recently, and this book is also a humble tribute to his memory. His legacy is large enough to include every chair imaginable, like the ones mentioned in this text. Some of them are featured in this *Chairpedia*. Others are manifestos of the Radical Design he practiced in 1974 that never made it into a sales catalogue, such as the monumental Lassù (which means "up there" in Italian), a chair conceived in a way that makes it impossible to sit on. Finally, he redesigned others that were already famous examples of the "anti-design" philosophy of Studio Alchimia—which, for that very reason, have paradoxically become part of the history of design—like his reinterpretation of Gio Ponti's Superleggera (1978), the iconic Proust armchair, and Joe Colombo's 4867 chair (1978), which he also redesigned. These three models are specifically mentioned in the book *Chairs. Historia de la silla* by Anatxu Zabalbeascoa (Editorial Gustavo Gili, 2018), originally published by Andreu World.

The *Chairpedia* initiative was launched by Andreu World in 2016, when it began compiling chair-related texts by writers and historians in an attempt to promote and publicize the history and culture of the chair. An open-ended project to be continued in the future, the first instalment has been materialized in this book published by La Fábrica to mark the company's 65th anniversary.

Authors

Antonio Solaz has spent half a lifetime handling Andreu World's corporate graphic design—since 1996, to be precise—a demanding job that occasionally gives him opportunities to demonstrate his artistic talent. In this book, he's found his paradise. A master of many creative techniques, he took pleasure in using them to illustrate each of these stories. Solaz is one of Spain's finest illustrators, yet his work is little known outside of Valencia. His father, Ismael Solaz, was a modern furniture designer whose creations (among them chairs and seats) won several awards in the 1970s. He had a strong influence on Antonio, who studied history and decoration at the Valencia School of Arts and Crafts before going into graphic communications and photography. All that experience and all those years working among chairs explain his matchless drawing skills.

Ramón Úbeda began to write about design and its stories in the 1980s, when he was editor-in-chief of *De Diseño* and *ARDI* magazines. He's continued to do so in all sorts of national and international publications, from *El País Semanal* to *Frame*, and in books like this one. His relationship with Andreu World began in 2005 with *Chairs*, the book written to celebrate the firm's 50th anniversary and published by RBA. Ten years later, it continued with *Historias para leer sentado*, which planted the seed of this *Chairpedia*. Since then, he has published *Chairs, historia de la silla* with Anatxu Zabalbeascoa in 2018 (Editorial Gustavo Gili), and the restaurant guide *Comer bien sentado* with Álvaro Castro in 2019 (Planeta Gastro). He is currently working on new publishing projects for the brand.

Authors

María José Balcells BA in Art History, is an expert on contemporary art and design. She manages the historical documents collection at the Research Center of the Museu del Disseny, Barcelona.

Pages 80, 84, 86, 88, 112

Santi Barjau has a PhD in Art History from the University of Barcelona. An expert on poster art from the first half of the twentieth century and Catalan Modernist architecture, he currently works at the Historical Archive of the City of Barcelona.

Pages 26, 36, 78, 108, 190

Isabel Campi is an industrial designer with a BA in Art History and a PhD in Design from the University of Barcelona. She curates exhibitions, writes articles, and has authored several books on the theory and history of design. She is the chairperson of Fundación Historia del Diseño.

Pages 54, 94, 130, 172, 196

Guillem Celada graduated from the University School of Industrial Design (ESDi) and completed the Master's in Research in Art and Design (MURAD) course at EINA, the University School of Art and Design, Barcelona. His work focuses on recovering elements and stories from the recent past of design.

Pages 58, 100, 118

Daniel Cid has a PhD in Art History. He worked as professor, academic director, and later scientific director at ELISAVA, the University School of Design and Engineering, Barcelona. He is currently an associate professor at the Winchester School of Art, University of Southampton.

Pages 186, 188, 194

Ana Domínguez has a BA in Art History with a concentration in Design from the Sotheby's Institute of Art, London. She is an exhibition curator and writes regularly for a number of national and international publications.

Pages 56, 104, 114, 132, 152, 154, 156, 176, 218, 220

José María Faerna is an art historian, editor, and journalist. He teaches occasionally, ran the magazine *Diseño Interior* for ten years, and writes regularly on art, architecture, and design for different media.

Pages 52, 192, 198, 202, 204

Albert Fuster is an architect with a PhD in Art History and Architecture from the ETSAB-UPC, Barcelona. He is the academic director of the ELISAVA design school. He has lectured at conferences and published articles on the connections between literature and architecture, which was also the subject of his doctoral thesis.

Pages 60, 64, 68, 122, 128

Marisa García Vergara is an architect with a PhD in the History and Theory of Architecture from the Polytechnic University of Catalonia. She currently teaches architectural composition at the University of Girona. Her research focuses on the relationship between art, design, and modern urban and architectural culture.

Pages 96, 98, 168

Daniel Giralt-Miracle is a critic, art historian, and professor. Former director of the Museu d'Art Contemporani, Barcelona (MACBA), he was the general curator of the International Year of Gaudí in 2002. From 2011 to 2018 he sat on the Cultural Council of the City of Barcelona.

Pages 38, 48, 72, 76, 222

Rosina Gómez-Baeza graduated from the University of Cambridge with a BA in English Language and Literature and studied Education Science at the London Polytechnic and the History of Art and French Civilization at the Catholic University of Paris. She was director of the ARCO fair from 1986 to 2006 and of LABoral from 2006 to 2011. She is currently a founding partner of YGB ART.

Pages 164, 166, 174

Pilar Mellado earned her PhD from the Polytechnic University of Valencia in the Industrial Project Design, Production, and Management doctorate program. Her doctoral thesis was a study and analysis of Pedro Miralles's work.

Page 102

Authors

Oriol Pibernat is a historian and researcher of material culture. He is currently a professor at EINA, the university school he directed from 1999 to 2016. He has authored articles and books on design, edited catalogues, and curated a variety of exhibitions.

Pages 34, 142, 146, 184, 210

Mónica Piera has a PhD in Art History from the University of Barcelona and completed the Works of Art course at the Sotheby's Institute of Art, London. She is an independent scholar. Nowadays she chairs the Association for Furniture Studies, an association that works to preserve and promote furniture heritage.

Pages 66, 110, 208

Isabel del Río as a degree in Product Design, as well as a BFA and MA in Advanced Art History Studies from the University of Barcelona. She teaches design history, theory, and criticism. She also researches objects for institutions such as Fundación Historia del Diseño and the Museu del Disseny, Barcelona.

Pages 24, 50, 62, 158, 160

Patricio Sáiz is a professor at the Autonomous University of Madrid and an expert on the history of industrial property and innovation. He has authored numerous books and articles and founded an international research network devoted to this topic: ibcnetwork.org.

Page 206

Carmen Sevilla is a professor of design history and theory at the University School of Art and Design, Valencia, and of design aesthetics at Jaume I University, Castellón. She has directed two design schools and combines teaching with her own creative work.

Pages 92, 126, 134, 138, 216

Rosalía Torrent is a full professor of art theory and aesthetics at Jaume I University, Castellón, and director of the Museu d'Art Contemporani Vicente Aguilera Cerni (MACVAC) in Vilafamés. Her research focuses on themes related to contemporary art, industrial design, and gender studies.

Pages 70, 82, 136, 144, 178

Mauricio Wiesenthal is a writer, enologist, and photographer of German descent. He has taught and lectured at different universities. An author of narratives, essays, and biographies, he has also edited several encyclopedic works.

Pages 9, 10, 11, 12, 13, 14, 15

Andreu World is a family business that has spent 65 years developing a solid industrial culture based on the production of high-quality, genuinely comfortable seats and tables for corporate and public workspaces, outdoor settings, hotels, coffee shops, and restaurants. It works with internationally renowned designers and architects such as Patricia Urquiola, Jasper Morrison, Alfredo Häberli, PearsonLloyd, and Lievore Altherr Molina. Good design, production capacity, and commitment to sustainability are the pillars of its corporate identity. The company has promoted an environmentally responsible production culture, which allows it to manufacture products using only wood from its own responsibly cultivated and replanted forests certified by the FSC® (Forest Stewardship Council).

Andreu World is currently one of the leading companies in the furniture industry and a major exporter of contemporary, avant-garde designer seats and tables. It is part of the Leading Brands of Spain Forum, an alliance of Spanish companies whose brands are well-known in the international arena. It has showrooms in Spain, Europe, the United States, and Asia and distributors in more than ninety countries.

Since 2001, the company has organized an International Design Contest that has become one of the longest-running design competitions in the world, with tens of thousands of entries. In addition to Spain's National Design Prize, over the years Andreu World has received other prestigious international distinctions, including the Red Dot Design Award, the ADI Design Index, Best of NeoCon Awards, and the Wallpaper Design Award.

Andreu World
C/ Los Sauces, 7
Urb. Olimar
46370 Chiva-Valencia
Tel. +34 96 180 57 00
www.andreuworld.com

Published by
Andreu World
La Fábrica

**Editorial Project
and Direction**
Ramón Úbeda

**Illustrations and
graphic design**
Antonio Solaz

Texts
María José Balcells
Santi Barjau
Isabel Campi
Guillem Celada
Daniel Cid
Ana Domínguez
José María Faerna
Albert Fuster
Marisa García Vergara
Daniel Giralt-Miracle
Rosina Gómez-Baeza
Pilar Mellado
Oriol Pibernat
Mónica Piera
Isabel del Río
Patricio Sáiz
Carmen Sevilla
Rosalía Torrent
Ramón Úbeda
Mauricio Wiesenthal

Copyeditors
Álvaro Villa
Isabel García Viejo

Translations
Art in Translation

Production
Adriana Rodríguez

Printers
Artes Gráficas Palermo

ISBN 978-84-17769-29-1
Legal Deposit: M-5626-2020

© Of the texts: their authors
© Of the illustrations: his author
© 2020 for the English edition:

La Fábrica
C/ Verónica, 13
28014 Madrid
Tel. +34 91 360 13 20
edicion@lafabrica.com
www.lafabrica.com